MOSAIC OF TWO MINDS

Gill Kingsland and Rhiannon Hopkins

Dedicated to the Small Stones online writing group, where the pieces of this mosaic first came together. Also to Satya Robin of the Amida Mandala Buddhist Temple, in Malvern, Worcestershire who began the Small Stones group in 2013. It quickly became a safe place to share joys, woes and things we would never have written without the support of a group of fellow writers who became trusted friends. With love and hopes for a long, prosperous and creative future.

THE INTRO

This book began as a concept*, which sounds rather grande for something with its roots in a slightly drunken lunch with two writers telling stories to each other across the wine bottle. These stories survived both the passing of time and sobriety, so we thought we should do something with them. We married them together with poetry and passing thoughts, fragments, the fascinating detritus that writers files - mental and actual - collect and sent them out into the world in this book.

We hope you enjoy this Mosaic of Two Minds. Can you see the joins?

Gill K and Rhiannon H

Cornwall 2018.

WANDERING WIT: FOOT-PRINTS OF AN INTROVERT MIND

RHIANNON HOPKINS

LEE ON THE SOLENT

The Bait Digger

On the empty beach,
In the last fading daylight,
the bait digger is at work.
In the close by streets,

on the roads and in the houses,

people live their technology driven lives,

Out here,

in the silent emptiness,

he uses a tool which would be

familiar to his grandfather,

to dig up the sand,

still damp from the just receding tide

and pick out long worms,

drop them into a bucket,

with all the solemnity and purpose

of an arcane ritual performed,

as a last sliver of the old moonrises over

the water,

idling on her back.

Winter Beach

Summer visitors do not know this beach.

Solitary stretch of sand and shingle.

Dusk tugging at the edges of the sky

at only six o clock

When the summer visitors return

the beach will wear a face,

less lonely.

For now there is only the dog and I,

two dedicated kite surfers

and the gulls whose cries,

like age old lamentations,

Are not enough to fill

the grand emptiness.

The Walk Home

In the eldritch half light,
we leave the road
and descend,
stony staircase,
muddy footpath,
to the empty beach in the gloaming.
Standing motionless on a shingle bank,
momentarily one with
the magnificent solitude
of pebbles, grey sand
and the ebbing
shushing sea.
The lights on the distant island
and over at Fawley Refinery
alone attest to life.
We mark our homeward path
with a track of boot and paw prints
in the sand.
A blackbird begins to pipe his farewell
to the day
in clear sharp notes
that make a cleft in the silence.

Seen at a Distance

Kite surfers on the Solent.

Sails of orange and azure, red and lime green.

From a distance it looks as though England

Has been visited by a flock

of giant, exotic migratory birds.

Summoning the Past

Walking barefoot on the beach
opens a door that leads back to
that childhood treat -
a day at the seaside.

A bucket and spade,

fish and chips at a promenade cafe,
some money to spend on tacky souvenirs in the gift
shops-
snow globes were my favourite -
and then the train ride home,
sleepy,
still clutching the bucket and spade,
all responsibility resting on adult shoulders.

A Passing Thought

This afternoon walking by the beach at Lee on the Solent, a rather strange solitary figure, dressed in a black wetsuit with striking blonde hair, was propelling himself along on a board, like a surfboard only flat, with a single oar. I had a kind of mad revisioning of Coleridge: In a burst of desperation the ancient mariner tore the albatross from round his neck, wrenched the cabin door from its hinges, threw it overboard then, grabbing an oar, followed it over the side and paddled away from the cursed ship as fast as he could

BIRD WATCHING

Hawk

Grey, hunched, motionless,
the bird stands beneath the trees.
Telescopically shrunk into itself
like a heron,
though this is not heron country.
Then the bird takes flight.
No heron.
a goshawk.
flying low across the field.
In that moment the silent wood comes alive

as, like an army in rout,

every other bird
takes off from its roost in the wood,
a terrified, twittering mass.
At the far end of the path I look back
The goshawk stands alone,
in the centre of the field,
lordly and keenly observant

Mine all Mine

Crow in the road,
pecking at pizza
fallen from someone's shopping bag.
The 5a bus comes around the corner

but crow will not leave his prize

and waits till the last minute,

only flying away when he is almost under the
wheels.

18/10/13

A murmuration of starlings rises
from the field,
dark specks against the blue black sky.
Playing avian follow my leader,
they rise and fall in perfect formation,
the only moving things in the still, late autumn
landscape.

17/10/13

Crow bathing in a puddle,
spraying the water with a flurry of wings,
droplets on his feathers that catch the sun
are like pearls on black velvet.

The Magpie Gavotte

Magpie strutting on the lawn,
a second magpie flutters down
and they face each other,
heads bob,
tails quiver.
The question has been asked -
do you want to dance? -
and answered -
yes-
and so they strut together

The Show Offs

Two magpies strut and flutter,
jump from fence to fly up again,
chattering and full
of self -importance.

Barrel chested pigeon

watches the display,

unmoving,

like an elderly uncle

watching the attention seeking antics

of two adolescents.

Herald of Summer

Was that …?
The sound stops me,
midway through typing a message.
Did I hear a …?
Listen carefully and -

yes,

it is.

Distant but clear,

the two note,

onomatopoeic ,

call:

cuckoo

cuck-oo.

Observing the Scenery

In the damp, empty park
black headed gull struts, surveys,
and makes throaty comments on
all that he sees

As the Season Changes

The pied wagtail hops and bobs along the pavement,
pausing to peck at dropped morsels from passers by.
Hello again, little bird,
it's been many months since I saw you,

could it be that spring is following,
not so far behind?

23/11/13

Gulls gather on the breakwater,
and the fading daylight
paints bars of dull gold on the soft sighing waves of
the Solent

9/8/13

A wren lives in the tree outside my window.
This morning she provides a sound track for my
meditation.
A series of chirrups and whistles,
her comments on the awakening day.
She is not so musical when,
in a burst of avian annoyance,
she scolds the local cats.
She is shrill as she
warns the other birds out of her territory,
letting them all know despite her size,
this wren is not to be messed with.

PROSE FRAGMENTS:1

Encounter

She comes to me and says –I have no fire
wood.
She has no firewood because she did not
gather any.
I cannot turn her away. She's afraid of the
forest.
She asks me why she is afraid and she's
like a small girl asking questions with
answers she has not the power to
understand. This crone who could be my
grandmother's grandmother, ancient,
gnarled, twisted as those trees she
fears.

I tell her – I have no idea why you are
afraid.
She says- you write books, you are
supposed to have the answers.

If only it were that simple.

Who sent you to me? I ask.
No one sent me, I came.
But why to me?
Because you live farthest from the forest.
It has no power to hurt you.
So anyone would say who does not know the
stories.
Tell me the stories.
They are old.
Tell me the stories.
I cannot, the words no longer exist.

I give her firewood, she gives me a Russian
blessing.
I do not see her again.

FIFTEEN SHORT PIECES

A Parable Of The Imagination

No one told me
girls cannot be pirates,
so imagination was a beast without fetters,
a bear that danced just because
it felt the sun on its fur.

And there really were unicorns -
and dragons.

And somewhere Rumplestiltskin
still hops up and down in fury
because the miller's daughter
has finally guessed his name.

19/1/14

Notebook records -
long ago train journeys
meetings with time faded lovers,
places and people to be filed under Then.
A curve in the arc of a life

that comes to rest in this quiet lamp lit room,

in the moment of now.

Soundscape

Clattering helicopter blades,
Cat snoring,
Fridge humming,
Wren scolding,

Clock ticking.

Soundtrack to morning
meditation.

From Another Country

On the bottom shelf of the bedside cabinet,
a small cardboard box containing
- omeprazole, tamoxifen, diflucan.

Names like the litany of a faith

practised in the very different country
of Chemo.
I drop the boxes of pills into a carrier bag.
Tomorrow I shall ask the pharmacist
to dispose of them.
On my way to the bin with the box I pause
and reflect,
with wonder and gratitude,
on the fact of my survival.

20/1/14

A sash of mist girdles the park
in the early morning,
leafless branches look like
they are suspended in mid air.

22/1/14

A fine spring like morning,

the cat dozes on the windowsill

in the first sun for many weeks,

next to George Orwell

who is drying out after

taking a swan dive into the bath.

14/11/13

A day that began with frustration,
and ended with friendship.
The days circle closing
with a ticking clock
and a snoring cat.

30/11/13

10.45 pm
the clock speaks its monotonous, sonorous
tick, tick, tick.
Curled in my lap the dog twitches a paw,
chasing dream rabbits
Into our comfortable,
lamp lit, enclosed space,
comes a reminder
of the life lived in the dark
beyond the windows,
as a fox begins to call
with a high, trembling yelp.

27/6/13

Listening to Gordon Lightfoot singing about his
Dream Street Rose.
The music that gave him a sense of narrative,
that's woven into the soundtrack of her life,
and connects them both with his long lost father.
Jim Croce tells his lost love It Doesn't Have to be
That Way,
music from her childhood.

They share wine and crisps

and memories of granddad,

as the summer evening draws itself out
toward night.

30/7/13

Early evening.
Lentils simmering,
Bizet's toreadors marching,
and the rain against the half open window,
has a strange metallic smell

For Mildred

You are the place
it begins.
The centre of the spiral
from which
questions radiate.
I ask them
knowing there can be
no answers.

For you I hold
empty space
at the heart

Nature's Gift

A blizzard of white blossoms cascades down.
covering the pavement,
swirling through the air,
carried by the breeze

to lie snowflake like upon the grass

in a blanket covering,

And still more falls.
The profligacy of heaven

Finely Balanced

Winter storms sent

tiles toppling,

fences falling.

But the nest

in the vee of the oak's

highest branches

remains perfectly balanced.

Birdbrained.

Not such an insult after all.

2/11/13

Squirrel perches on the tree branch,

that came down in last week's storm,

thick bush of tail hanging down

like the stole falling

from the shoulder of a 1940's movie star.

1/2/14

All afternoon -
while writing,
while cooking,
while reading -
rain has beat its rhythm on the window,
now fierce and intense,
now gentler, sporadic,
as if it might be stopping soon.
But no.
It is now one a m
and still the rain drum
beats

LANDSCAPE

The Watcher

The wood is not deserted as it appears.
As we come down the path,

we have been seen by an unseen watcher.

The deer runs from the trees

leaping over a fallen log,

graceful as no mere athlete could be .

She stops in the shelter of tangled brush,

brown velvet coat perfect camouflage,

watching,

alert,

ready to run again if we turn in her direction.

20/7/13

We went in search of the sea,

my son, the dog and I.

He saw it first.

That single blue line of

water-sky,

place where element and heavens meet,

as if the world has neat seams at its edges.

2/5/13

We walk the empty fields in the almost sunset time,
serenaded by birdsong,
embraced by summer-like warmth,
just seeping from the day.
By the broken down fence.

bluebells,

delicate as a pianists fingers picking out
the last notes of a Chopin etude.

Connection

Following the rutted path that runs

between fields of green corn.

Stepping in the footprints of a child

who has never been here,

crossing the stile she

has never climbed over.

She meets me in the open spaces,

of field and wood,

and takes me to

the home that is gone.

The Afternoon Walk

Louring blue black sky,

foraging crows black against green grass

of fields still awaiting the plough's first kiss.

Ramshackle barn of corrugated tin,

dulled silver, orange rust,

and further away the red tiled roofs

of Collingwood naval base.

On the far edge of the field silver pylons

like giants with arms spread in supplication

to strange gods.

And the only sounds are the voices of the wind,

telling the stories it alone knows,

and the whisper rustle of grass

brushing against my boots.

23/3/14

The birds in the wood were singing,
clear notes, sweet notes.
Singing up the green shoots,
singing up the new grass,
singing up the young leaves,
singing up the rising sap.

The birds in the wood were singing
clear notes, sweet notes.
Singing up Spring.

The Coming King

Winter hides his eyes but
his chill breath betrays him,
there behind
Autumn's russet and crimson petticoats
decorated with berries,
horse chestnuts
and strands from dark Lady Evergreen
who gives no care for any season.

Autumn wears her yellow crown,
curtseys to Old Father Sun
who smiles benignly,
sheds warmth momentarily
on the solitary dog walker
following the path to the sea.

Autumn's dance is but
a farewell masquerade
and Old Father Sun has turned
his most radiant smile on
other lands now
because Winter is the coming king.

25/11/13

SUNDAY EVENING

In the twilight we follow the path across the field,
skirting the muddiest patches.
Crows give out their hoarse, throaty goodnight cho-
rus.
On the bridge I pause, look back
at the empty land under the fading light,
silent now and full of shadows.
Whistle to the dog busy investigating something in a
bush
and we follow the path to the village,
to home,
and cheese on toast
with a cup of hot strong tea for me
and bacon flavoured biscuit for dog.

2/10/13

After the children are in school
and the sorority of Dog Walking Mothers
has dispersed,
the park waits

like a house prepared for visitors
yet to arrive.
Empty benches invite no one.
Horse chestnut trees,
turning crisp gold,
drop their harvest of dark brown conkers
onto the grass.
Gulls investigating litter
stalk the perimeter of
the chained off cricket pitch.
Crows pick their way across the grass,
stately as Elizabethan courtiers.
Nothing else moves.
(Conts)

Then the old man with the little papillon
comes from the path beside the community
centre,
a child runs into the playground to climb the
slide,
and a terrier splits the morning silence
with a delighted bark as her ball is thrown.

17/11/13

Summer sang her last song today,
casting light and what warmth remained in her over
the dull chilly morning.
In the light and shade patterns

on the floor of the wood she sang a promise

-I will come again,I will come again.

The dove added its repetitive verse-

coo, coo, coo, coo.

Our long shadows preceded us down the footpath.

And when the sun kissed the weathered limbs
of the three ancient oak trees in the centre of the field
it sang that same refrain -
I will come again, I will come again.

A Moment

A rook flies lazily, wings barely moving,

on his way home to see the wife and kids.

Bluebells and cow parsley grow in the hedgerow

and the air is heavy with a lush green smell.

Birdsong in the wood,

distant sounds of a cricket match

on the recreation ground,

and a church bell tolling

for evening service.

A summer Sunday evening in England.

PROSE FRAGMENT: 2

Written on York Railway Station

I feel my individuality on late night railway stations. In the yellow light, hugged inside my coat against the cold, I wait with my fellow passengers. Each face a story, each story a life. They have their reasons for travelling as I have mine, dream of their homes as I do mine – a single room with faded cream wallpaper and an old gas fire. Perhaps loved ones are waiting for them. I live solitary by choice.

Waiting on the platform, unknown, unre-marked, but still vitally me. We are English so we do not pass the time in conversation, nor even make eye contact. If the train is late, it is acceptable to grumble to the old man in the fur hat or the stout woman in the tweed skirt and yellow jacket about the iniquities of the rail-way system. But as it is we remain with inches of concrete and centuries of custom holding us apart.

Uniquely me, uniquely him, uniquely her.

Waiting for a train, waiting to be carried back to lives where we're known and, though always separate, my individual self merges with an-other. But on late night railway stations I stand solitary, the only me in the entire world and completely unknown.

A MISCELLANY

In Memoriam

Remembrance Day 2014

We gathered with lighted candles.

The names were read aloud -

from Adams to Lock

from Longman to Young.

At the moment when a politician saw

"the lights going out all over Europe"

one hundred years ago

the candles were extinguished.

We stood in semi darkness.

Our silence an arc

of prayer and reflection,

from an English Village

to former French battlefields,

where it found and blessed the lost bones

of its sons and daughters.

Rescue

The bee had tumbled into the dog's water bowl.
He was at the very edge struggling to lift himself
clear but there was nothing to give him purchase.
A human provided the needful.

He clambered onto the proffered stick.

You could imagine the sigh of relief

as he was elevated above what was almost

his watery grave.

He sat upon the stick drying in the sun,

rubbing himself with his back legs

as a cat will rub its face when grooming.
Then suddenly he flew,

sailing away across the garden,

into the summer day

2/6/13

I built an igloo of words
A refuge against
the Polar Bears of mediocrity,
An ice palace for
my feared and treasured self.
A place where fragile dreams can safely rest,
Dance with possibility,
while their wings grow strong,
as a butterfly's at first unfolding.

18/5/13

Rhyming couplets twirl in my head
but it is late, I want to go to bed.
Words they dance and sing and fight,
oh, do please keep still
and let me say goodnight.
They turn and twist and fidget and prance
but this old owl don't wanna dance.
It's just no good, the words jump faster,
trying to sleep would be a disaster.
So I marshal those words in some order on a
page, now will you kindly leave the stage?

Becoming

Talk to me about the lost things,

the never found things,

of water under the bridge

and that place beyond the rainbow's end.

Speak as the voice of many rivers,

of clouds and distances crossed and calamities met

and avoided.

Tell me tales of truth, gentle lies,

and confessions whispered in dusty midnight rooms

to no one.

Spin old tales from new yarn

so I may know what it is to be the woman who lives

in this skin.

Just Suppose...

What if -
None of it mattered?
Not the Life Affecting stuff,
just all those little worries that are
crumbs in your mental bed,
preventing you from settling.

What if -
Your perpetual train of thought took a detour?
Instead of running daily from The Habitual to
Acquired Custom via Tried and Tested,
it went down the branch line that leads to
New Ways of Seeing,
The Unfamiliar,
or even
Things I Have Never Considered Before,.

What if -
instead of just waking up in the morning
you spent all day Waking Up?

What if...?

13/6/13

A wet Wednesday in June.
Slip, slide, slosh through the wood,
damp dog walking.
Swish, sweep, swish of windscreen wipers,

a passenger with a friend driving.
Drip, drip, drip, from the roof of a railway station,
newspaper strewn train, a dry cocoon while travelling.

Staccato spattering of drops against glass,

warm communal space with friends, coffee, talking

Puddled streets and sodden gardens

the walk home I am expecting.

Rush and fall of water into drains,
an offer of a lift as the day is ending.

4/6/13

We pass the garage door with the peeling,
chipped red paint,

the house with the torn sofa dumped in the
garden,

the turning down to the green where children
are playing cricket.

Heading home after a ramble through summer
fields.

Sunlight polishes the paintwork of a black car,

sunlight polishes the paintwork of a red car.

Exchange a smile with a neighbour I cannot be
said to know,

cut across empty parking bays to the gates,

where I unclip the dog's lead,

fish in my pocket for keys,

open the gate,

the dog runs to wait on the doorstep while I un
lock the door.

This is home - for now.

6/6/13

I stood in front of the huge clock,
with the £450 price tag.
My god! What a thing!
"It's majolica," the shop assistant said.
"It's a monstrosity," I responded -
civility never having been more important to me than
honesty.

The clock, all of two feet high,
is decorated in yellow and green,
that stops at the borders of garish -
but not so far that it cannot see across.
At the base of the central clock face,
two peacocks in blue and green.
Above it, crowning the whole edifice,
a pair of stags heads in cinnamon brown, antlers
spread.

My god! What a thing!

Ophelia Passing

Storm Ophelia trailed her skirts across

southern England.

The sky turned a dull and dusty yellow,

as if Miss Havisham's decaying wedding veil

had been dropped over the day.

And in the eerie, alternate twilight

a hush,

a sense of waiting.

The countryside held its breath

to watch Ophelia passing.

You've Got, Junk, Mail

On opening my junk mail folder I find I am a very popular girl. Miss Darlana Ibrahim of Burkina Faso is impressed to be seeking her soul mate and like to be in relationship with me. Hang on, pet, you've got competition. Julia has read my profile on a site I have never been on and wants to get to know me, she is sure we'd be "soooo" good together and a couple of sex dating websites want to give me immediate hookups with, respectively, "hotties" or Wild Girls - I'll certainly pass on the latter, they sound scary!!

Anyway, I can pick and choose now because I am wealthy. You see, a Kenyan widow who is dying of cancer wants to share her fortune with me just for help in getting it out of the country PLUS I

have won a lottery I never bought a ticket for -
clever of me, huh?

 The only thing of no use to me at all are the
offers of cheap Viagra. Mind you, there is that
droopy plant in the kitchen, perhaps a wee blue
pill or two might perk it up?

The Introvert Has a Busy Week.

Day one: interacting with the world has the
charm of novelty.

Day Two: edgy but coping. Steering toward the moment when she gets on the bus and heads home.

Day Three: feeling excavated, extracted from the
deep mines of solitude and placed in a display.
A kind of human Koh-i-Noor.

Day Four: headachy, slightly nauseous, longing for
the sofa with a cup of tea a book and the dog. Her
life behind the closed door.

Praise be to god there is to be no day five.

Life Symphony

(1)

Skylarks singing in a summer sky,
eight year old girl in a gingham dress
craning her neck to look for them.
Mum singing Jerusalem over the washing
up,
while the girl sits at the table colouring.
The clatter she and her brother made
as they stomped around in dustbin lid
shoes
and pigs snuffling, grunting, squealing,
familiar background sounds.
Falling asleep to the sound of combine
harvesters on late summer evenings when
it was still light at nine o clock.
And TV theme tunes -
Z Cars, Dr Who, Blue Peter, Robinson
Crusoe.
Ice cream van chimes,

lawnmowers on still Sunday afternoons,
the clatter of a five barred gate swinging
shut
and footsteps on the gravel path
of an English churchyard.

(2)

The songs of the innocent days of the churchyard wall.
The songs of the dark time when the music
was the only refuge.
The songs of the brief happy period of
the marriage she knew to be a mistake from the
start. The one good to come from the mistake, a
beloved son.

His voice as he came through the door
in his father's arms, reaching for her and saying
"mummy" for the first time.
Other voices now stilled in death -

dad, 'stick the kettle on while you're there,
ducks."
Brenda Whateley, "you're like my second
daughter."
Sandra, "it's easy, just turn right in
France."
Voices of those with whom
contact has been lost,
memory's precious and semi precious
stones.

(3)

Sounds of places she has been:
The vaporetti in Venice,
the constant stream of traffic
on Kentish Town Road,
the swish and whisper of Sheffield's
trams.
The come and go bustle
of a hundred railway stations,
the come and buy patter of east end
market traders.

The grand hush of cathedrals and
the lonely piping call of waders
on the mud of a tidal river
where she walked every evening
of an Indian summer just a few years ago.

Sounds of places she has lived:
The chatter of children
mixing Punjabi and English
on the Limehouse estate
she would rather forget.
The Yorkshire accent
that has left its mark in her own voice,
church bells in a Gloucestershire village
the scream of seagulls in an English
seaside town,
the hush of rural Hertfordshire

Sounds of now:
the heavy breathing of a sleeping dog,
a ticking clock,

the echo of all those other sounds
as memory walks in the silence of an early
morning.

7/9/13

The door into the second hand bookshop is
narrow as a blade.
An electric bell announces your entry
into the dim and musty smelling interior-
it's like entering the pages of the books
themselves.
The narrow passage between high, crammed full
bookcases leads you to niches where shelves of
books line the walls and still more books are stacked
on the floor, spread on tables.
Nineteenth century bound Dickens, £40, shares
space with paperback Margaret Drabble, £2.50.
Military history and natural history fall easily
 together, philosophy and religion share a
bookcase,
mechanical engineering and chemistry form
alliance on the next shelf.

Bibliophile's heaven,
blissful refuge from a rainy afternoon
in Lewes.

27/7/13

Stubbington Park at Dusk.

The trick cyclists have all gone home for tea.
Tonight they will dream of cool moves
and well-impressed mates.
The games of football have all been declared
won, lost or drawn and someone
has taken his ball home.
The tribal gatherings of teenagers -
those rebels who all dress exactly alike -
the morning Sorority of Dog Walking Mothers,
the daytime walkers and loungers and
the en-route passers through
have all dispersed into
the surrounding streets
leaving behind them -
a plastic bottle here, a crisp packet there,
a disposable barbecue not disposed of.
(Conts)

There are only two frisbee players
watched by a woman on a disability scooter,
and a teenage couple
sitting on the grass, facing each other
as the dog and I
walk under the beech trees,
toward the old house with the Georgian façade
on the edge of the park.
Dog stops to investigate a discarded chip
wrapper
ignoring my command to "leave it",
the contraband is too tempting.
I whistle and she raises her head
as the sound finds its echo,
the sharp note causing a ripple
in the park's still, green tranquillity.

09/02/14

Stubbington Village

The library and the shops wear
their Sunday faces,

closed, empty, unlit.

Gulls swim in the centre

of the flooded park

and on the tennis court a man

practices his backhand.

The number 4 bus circles the roundabout,

waits with open doors at the stop but

collects no passengers

and no one alights.

We pass the pet shop-
the dog snuffles at the door,
scenting good things within.
We pass the closed down supermarket
and the Red Lion pub,

taking the longer way home.
Stubbington Lane to Bells Lane,
crossing from one to the other almost without
pause
meeting scant traffic on this damp grey after
noon,
just a few cars and a frowning cyclist.

The sky is darkening so we take the shortcut
past the Catholic church where
Mother Mary stands on her plinth in the
vestibule,
hands outspread in welcome or maybe
resignation.
As we reach Angelus Close
the rain begins again

PROSE FRAGMENT:3

Kirkwood

Over time he has swallowed plenty and now he's sick of it. Sick of all the vile and bitter things he has swallowed down in silence. Sick of the lies and double-dealing he has witnessed. Supremely sick of Doctor Elderwood's lust masquerading as Christian concern. He knows this community, this little town within a town; knows it all too well. Oh yes, my friends, he thinks, looking at the pale faces around him in the dining hall and the one darker Latin one, (Manuel, you're the most honest of the lot – only a cheat and at least an honest one.) I know you and if I opened my mouth and spewed out all I've swallowed what a vomiting that would be. What a vile, rich soup for you all to drown in.

"Damn the lot of you!"

He stands on a deserted hill and screams the words he dare not speak. They are powerful men. He fears them almost as much as he despises them. Their power could be broken. Crumble they might, but fall? He doesn't believe they ever will.

In desperation, he starts sending coded messages to the newspapers. Unsigned or with an alias pulled at random from the telephone book. In a week of this he has spanned the alphabet in leaps. Like the striding giant with the seven league boots from the fairy stories a woman read to him once when he was a child. (It could not have been his mother.) He had been Adams and Kingsley, Parsons and Williams. The book fell open when he knocked it off his desk and the giant took a step back – Bassett. The notes caused a ripple of amused speculation by a famous columnist. Clearly, the man had drinking buddies on rival papers and they had compared notes, he thought. In the end he was dismissed as a harmless crank.

"What else can I do?" He asked aloud. There was nothing here to answer him. The cream coloured walls of his study do not even give back an echo. The window is open, a breeze stirs the half pulled down blind. And a corresponding whisper stirs his agitated thoughts, sends up a mental dust cloud that settles into an answer – "tell the truth."

The truth? Crazy. These men, no matter where he went, no matter how far he travelled, would find him. The tentacles of the organisation spread to all the continents. Like a sodding great octopus poised over the globe, he thinks. And I have to stand up to that? Against that?

He goes to the chapel. Kneels before the altar and gazes up at the crucified Christ. His head is turned away. Busy dying for the sins of the world - (dying for those bastards and sons of bastards? How can that be?) He cannot even look a supplicant in the face. But he cannot pray. His mouth feels dry as dusty old manuscripts forgotten on a library shelf. (He doesn't want to think of the library – Elderwood's domain.)

The same woman who read him the fairy story folded his hands together and taught him to pray. A moment of kindness in a life otherwise devoid of even a loving smile. Celibate for all his 45 years. Too scared to say yes to the brazen hussies who wait like predators on Marlin Street, too respectful of every other woman. He stopped masturbating a long time ago and is sure he is now impotent. Even the thoughts don't come to him – thoughts of slim tanned

limbs in revealing bikinis on tropical islands.
Once his favourite fantasy. His strongest
feeling now is his rage; and that too is an impotent thing.

He looks again at the crucified Lord and thinks
of His cousin, John the Baptist. "I am the
voice of one crying in the wilderness." That is
what he should be. But John cried the coming
of good news. He is more like an old Roman
soothsayer studying the auguries in the entrails
of slain beasts, cry doom and disaster if we do
not change our ways.

The voice behind him makes him jump.
"I had a feeling I'd find you in here,"
And he has a murderous impulse to turn to face
Elderwood - and finish at least one of them
off.
No, no, careful, he admonishes himself. Don't
ever become as bad as they are.

WORLDS IN WET SAND: IDEAS OF A PARALLEL MIND

GILL KINGSLAND

Hay Rolls

Hayfields, the scent of grasses

Dried and cut

The harvest a celebration

If brought in before the rain

Each year the same

Hay to gather, but

No longer do hayricks

Rise

No longer are ricks roofed, woven

To rainproof protection

No stooks are stacked

Awaiting collection

Instead

Hayrolls

Plastic-covered

Sit like abandoned spring rolls

Around the field

Harvest Rolls,

Remnants of a picnic

Set out for the gods.

TUBULAR

He arrived, panting.

There it was, the tunnel, the link between the outside world and his homeland, the birth tunnel of his nascent modern state, the beginning of the end for their old ways, for their solitude, their traditions, their neutrality, their isolation, their peace and their independence.

There were those who had objected to its building, of course, seeing it as an intrusion, an invasion, as something that brought their doom. Perhaps they were right, for it had caused riots and protests in the towns as those for, and those against, the changes it would bring as well as the change of its mere existence, met and argued. It had been the cause of three blacked eyes, one premature birth and numerous incidences of drunkenness as people met in bars to discuss it. Such uprisings had been unknown for over two hundred years in his safe little country, tucked into its impenetrable valley. Yes, it was an intrusion, the tunnel, its purpose was to bring intruders into the land and unrest was to be expected with so many of the people so afraid and resentful of the strangers and the changes they would bring (already there were more restaurants, bars, hotels than ever before). But it would bring goods, much needed money and trade, new ideas, new technology, new opportunities. Through it would blow a much needed drench of fresher air; an even greater blessing than the trade in his mind for had they not been breathing the stale atmosphere of complacency, an oxygen tainted by the stagnation of their society, for years?

And now…this. His foot touched something; a discordant call drew his gaze down to the ravaged ground.

It was the Bell.

Once belonging to an old and crumbling church that had been recently rebuilt in the hope that it would show the people that the town Council both revered the old but were unafraid of the new, the Bell - full of the myth and tradition of its history – had been rehomed in a spire that marked the apex of the tunnel. The church had six new bells to peal while the Old Bell continued calling at daybreak, noon and nightfall as it had always done, so that those in the mountains should be aware of the time in the town for, as everyone knew, town and mountain time was different.

The mountains, looming high above his small country, had dictated life there for centuries – for too long perhaps? They had become, in a way, living legends surrounded by superstitions no-one wanted to question – if you live in avalanche country, they said, you don't shout so loud! Even the Old Bell had been muffled;

it whispered when it tolled for a passing and murmured its welcomes and congratulations for birth, new life and now, according to some, its celebration of their entrance into the Twenty First century. A slow and faltering entrance on unsteady baby-feet it may be, but an entrance nonetheless.

He drew a long breath. Whatever ideology it had tolled for, the Old Bell lay now croaking in its fractured voice as rocks and chunks of concrete moved against it. Half buried in the rubble around the tunnel's mouth, it was part of the spatter, of the remnant vomit that had spewed out after the explosion inside the hard-dug tube while he, in his boots, stood holding his jacket like a father waiting to mop up after his baby.

And why not?

After all had he not helped build this? Had his designs not been the egg that his money – and the money of others – had helped fertilise? He stood there and felt his child's pain. He felt a father's anger at those who had caused this pain. Around him men, from this country in which sat the open mouth of this new venture, from his own country, from America, France, England, Japan and many others who had been involved in the conception, the creation of his idea, men who had come to see this grand opening now found shovels and dug.

And talked.

A fault in the building?

A fault in the materials?

An undiscovered fault in the geology?

A fault…?

No fault, said one voice. No fault in any of it. This was built safely, built to last. This was no fault, no angry god, no cause for superstition. This was sabotage; be its origin in terrorism, in home grown political infighting – for the loss of this tubular investment in modernity could topple the young government, reinstate the old men, the men of tradition – or in some business race for the ores and minerals in their mountains, it was still sabotage.

He moved then, taking up his own tools, strapping on his yellow jacket, fitting his hard yellow helmet to his head and went to work beside the owner of that voice. There had been anger in it. And reason. A voice defending its own, defending the faith he had in his work.

He and the man who defended his child dug shoulder to shoulder, moving rubble, telling the machines to wait. Machines would tear and scar and cause more damage. This, in spite of the scale of the wound, needed careful excavation. They must not bring more of the mountain down on the train trapped in its bowels.

Finally, they heard a noise. A scraping, a cautious sound hidden within the sounds of fire, destruction, fear.

'Hello?' he called and faintly, in return, came a hoarse and painful cry,

'Allo? Allo?'

He dug with renewed ferocity and even more care, his nameless friend at his shoulder. He was aware of more men joining them, working either side of them, united in the effort of reaching those still living on the far side of the fall. When the emergency lighting failed they simply switched on the lights on their helmets, wedging the torches and lanterns they carried on their belts on handy rocks and ledges to light their work, and carried on digging until a small hole appeared. It was blocked almost immediately, before anyone could peer through, by a hand; a male hand, bloodied and muddied, digging back towards them. It flapped for a moment, lost in this experience of freedom, fingers still clawed, still in the habits of the past hours, trying to dig even though there was nothing for them to grasp and pull and fling. He touched them gently, watched them uncurl and then solemnly the two hands clasped and shook in greeting. He could hear its owner sobbing.

More men arrived. Still no machines for still it was far from safe for the diggers and drills to enter but the rubble was moved; other hands, those of men, women, children, appeared, voices were heard and answered to be followed by the bodies and faces of those they had freed. The train, they were told, was trapped, broken. There had been three explosions, one at this end, where the tunnel began, one in the middle and one at the other end, near the exit, near the station.

At the far end? he queried. Heads nodded. It would have gone off, then, he thought, near the spot where the dignitaries would be waiting to welcome these first official tourists, booked en-mass into the finest of the new hotels the building of the tunnel had made necessary – and among those dignitaries, would be his own father. Someone tapped his shoulder, one of the other diggers, a man he vaguely recognised as a Frenchman who had worked with him before, when the tunnel was still in its embryonic stages.

'They are saying,' he gestured to the people being led, or carried, away from the scene, their steps lit by bobbing torches, 'that there are many dead, even more injured. They say the air conditioning is blowing in cold air and fanning the flames, not sucking out smoke. They say it is this, rather than the bomb in-juries, that is killing people now.'

'If we can get to the controls…' coughed the man who had been working at his side, 'we might be able to switch it over. It might help.'

'We can try.' He nodded, 'In the meantime,' he said to the Frenchman, 'give the medics breathing kits and get them in to the injured as soon as you can.'

He watched for a second as people moved to do all that they could, and then turned, began to wriggle through the rubble, to slide down the other side into the black, choking space that was, for now, a tomb.

Or a battlefield.

'Amazing,' said a now familiar voice at his elbow, 'how a clever man can be so stupid.'

Breathing apparatus was thrust at him. He grinned sheepishly into the dark, fumbling to put it on and relight his torch.

'Thank you.' His lantern flared as he found and thumbed the switch, there was a loose connection there, he thought. He must attend to it.

'I'm sorry. It's just…my father would have been at the far end, meeting and greeting. I wanted to get through, to see if he is OK…he is an elderly man, stubborn. He wouldn't run.'

'It's OK. Now, are you ready? The first maintenance tunnel entrance should be around 100 yards on…'

They made their way across the broken tracks, crawling under the remains of a coach they dare not peer into and found part of the train wedged against the metal door.

'We'll have to try for the next entrance' he said, the groans and pleas for help in that hot, choking space lit only by spasmodic but vicious flames making him think of Dante's circles of hell. Muttering reassuring phrases, patting the hands that clutched at them, they pushed on, through and past the train. The next entrance was jammed too, the restaurant car was resting against it and a few people were climbing slowly out, helping each other, using napkins as bandages.

They left a torch with them, told them medical help was on its way and crawled under the carriage wheels.

'Next one might be clear,' he wheezed into his radio link.

'Optimist.' A single word that sounded tinny in his ears. It comforted him, made him chuckle as he pulled himself clear of the carriage.

There was no warning. Only a crash, a rumble, a falling of earth and stone and he was pinned in a small cave made of the wall and part of a carriage where it leaned sideways at an incredible angle.

'Are you alright?'

A hand groped for him.

'Ah, not sure. Dizzy. Head hurts, and my leg. You?'

'Not so bad. I'm bleeding but it doesn't seem to be anything too much. No arteries.'

They shuffled and groped carefully, finding each other in the dark.

'So, if we're going to be here a while, you could tell me your name.'

'Baertschi. Timo Baertschi.'

'Baertschi? Then your father is…'

'Rodolphe Baertschi. Ex prime minister, leader of the opposition,' he sighed wearily. 'The main targets of his distaste, this tunnel and his youngest son. Me, in fact. He really didn't want to be part of the welcoming committee but the government decreed it. He rather thought of it as an insult to him as a man but, being my father he did it with full pomp and ceremony. Or he would have done if there hadn't been this… What about you? If we are to be here, as you say, for a while I should know your name. And where you're from – there is something about your accent…'

'Solly. Solomon Rosemurgy. I'm British, but the accent, that comes from Cornwall. Generations of us have called that home, wherever we live. Generations of miners. My great-grandmother, she used to say, there may be a Cornish miner in every hole in the world, but there's a Rosemurgy in charge of 'em.'

'Tell me about your family, your great grandmother.'

He needed, he thought, a story just as he had loved as a child. Something to stir his imagination, to excite him. He must keep his blood pumping, he must stay awake, fight the desire to close his eyes.

'Oh, I can tell you stories about my Great-Grandmother, such stories we have in our family.'

'Really? You know about the people who were before you?'

'Of course. They still be family, even if they are dead now. Part of them is in you, making you what you are, who you are even though you grow away from them in the cycle of time and they from you. Roots are important, you should know that.'

'Like building a bridge – good foundations needed.'

'Exactly. Now, I'll tell 'ee about my foundations if you like, but don't get confused, because my Great Grandfather, he was a Solomon too. All the eldest sons are called Solomon.'

And Solly, as he stripped Timo's glove off and felt for his pulse, began to tell stories as his grandfather and his father had told them and as he spoke Timo felt as if the other Sollys had gathered to tell him their yarns; he could see the green grass and bright blue skies, see the dark of the mines and the mud and slurry of the sheds as Solomon called them forth for him.

*

'Back aways, my father would tell us, aways when my grandfather was small, my great grandfather Solomon was waiting for the birth of his second child…

…Solomon lit his pipe and settled on the wall that ran the length of the lane, squinting at the sky through his smoke. He breathed in appreciatively and thought of taking a walk, but… no…this was no time to be too far from his own door, not with his wife giving birth to their child there in the bed where he – or she – had been conceived. She had said nothing, at first, dishing up a meal and asking after his day and the men he worked with as she usually did, adding her concerns for his father who had seemed, she thought, to be in more pain than usual.

'Perhaps it is the damp that makes him ache so…' she was saying, then she had suddenly grasped her swollen belly and bent almost double over the stew-pot and he had caught her and half carried her away from the fire.

His father had nodded.

'I thought as much. Women get a certain look when it's their time. Now, don't you worry son, your mother will have everything under control. Don't half the women of Crowan come to her when their babes are due? And little Solly can stay with me.' He held out his hand to his firstborn grandson and smiled,

'Come alonga here, lad and I'll tell 'ee a tale. And don't worry about your Mamm, 'tis womens' work and she's an able woman.'

And little Solly had gone to his grandpa and climbed carefully into the well between the old man's bent thighs.

Soon afterwards with Jane, his wife, safely abed and his mother caring for her, with his father caring for the curious Solly he realised the proceedings had reached that stage when he had no place there. He was unwanted, in the way and irritated by his seeming uselessness.

Ah, but there was no point in worriting about that – he remembered it well enough when Solly was born, the needlessness of his presence.

'It's a woman's thing, it's other women she needs right now. She'll need you later. All things in their time, boy. Remember that and make no grudges over it.' His father had said, and he had been right.

Still, it didn't stop a man fearing the thing that lay on the other side of birth. He worried about his wife, saw a nightmarish vision where he lost both her and the child, where he had to stand at their graveside on a day of grey mizzle and see them buried in the dank Cornish earth while young Solly cried into his shoulder.

At first he had thought to walk off this false premonition, for of course nothing like that would happen, not with God and his Mamm looking after Jane and the child. So he had set off at a spanking pace down the lane but after a few steps had slowed, hesitated, looked back. He could still see his door, and the setting sun like red gold, reflecting in the glass of the windows and it had, somehow, seemed wrong to go beyond that point.

So he hoisted himself onto the wall, feeling the warm stone beneath him, hearing the rasping brush of grass and wildflowers against his boots, smelling the salt of the sea just a mile or two away over the fields.

He sighed.

He would sit here, keep watch over his family, take time to taste the sweet evening air and that would be enough. That, for a man who spent his days at the bal, in the blackest of the shafts where silence was rare and the knockers were always hovering at the brink of awareness and shadows blacker than the darkness of the mines flitted from corner to corner, tunnel to tunnel, all in that moment before seeing, was a blessing.

He looked back towards his home, watching his son hanging onto his grandmother's skirts as she gathered in freshly laundered sheets, relieved, he could tell, at getting them dry for they would be needed before the night was out. She paused at her flower beds, breathing in their scents and plucking a handful of mint, a few sprigs of thyme as she passed.

She loved her herbs, her flowers, his Mamm, Solomon thought as he watched her shake out a shift, a brilliant white cotton shift for his Jane to wear once the hard work was done and she was made comfortable again. No neighbouring dog, cat, chick or child had ever dared root those plants out and there they grew, strong and brilliant but out of place in that little patch in front of the cottage. Twern't a garden. Twern't by rights even theirs, that patch. But no-one dared to argue over their right to use it and plant it.

No-one argued with his Mamm. Not his Pa, not the mine agents, not the foremen, not the mine owners who let these cottages to their workers, no one. Not even when she'd been working up at Wheal Abraham mine would anyone gainsay her. She was a fearsome one, even then, he thought fondly with a touch of complacent pride.

She'd started there when she was about eight, walking to and from with her Pa and her brothers, spending her days separating the ore from the waste and then walking home again. By the time she was twelve she was in the dressing sheds, spalling with style – no-one broke the large stones with such a swing on that long-handled hammer as young Mary Rogers, they said and her cobbing was a joy to watch; neat and nimble-fingered as she was the short hammer broke the waste from the ore with a rhythmic efficiency. Or so his Pa said. His Mamm rarely spoke of her time in the sheds as a Bal Maiden, one of the women who broke, sorted and washed the ore and, like most she had left the mine once she married.

Ah, there was a story from his childhood… how Pa met Mamm over Uncle James' broken leg!

It was one of father's favourite stories for a winter's night around the fire.

'They called me Solly, my name being Solomon and too big a name, the older men said, for a sprat like me.' He would begin, with a sparky look at the young Solomon, sitting at his feet. 'But I was a well grown sprat…'

He had been, he would say, broad shouldered and strong with a stride that spanned the Tamar, as if anyone believed that!

'Well, on this day I'd been going down into the shaft with the others on my shift. With us was a lad, barely past his twelfth birthday, with a shock of dusty dark hair and eyes as black as the devil's own. And he was a bad 'un. Not real bad, mind, but always up to mischief, he was. His name was James Rogers. His sister Mary worked in the dressing sheds, a pretty girl with the same dark hair and wicked black eyes and, when she was scrubbed up of a Sunday, you could admire her clear, pale skin that looked like cream and velvet.'

His Pa's eyes always took on a faraway look here, as he remembered that church with him singing his hymns and dreaming of stroking a tender finger across the curve of his Mary's jaw, right to that dent that was not quite a dimple in the centre of her cheek. A dent that flickered when she smiled and gave away her own awareness of his look.

'Aye, a pretty lass, your mother. Always was, always will be…' he'd say with a flick of a grin as his mother passed his chair with her stern face a little softer as she touched his shoulder, and you could see a ghost of the prettiness Pa spoke of as he sat with his pipe and his ale.

'James, being new to being underground and showing off to hide the fact he were scared, he mucked about as we went down and fell of'n ladder. Well, I were there, and knew the lad, so it fell to me to bring 'un out. He weren't mortal, but he'd broke his leg good and proper. So I put him across me shoulders and hoisted him out of it.'

'A thousand feet or more down, they were. Your Pa carried your Uncle James straight up and into the light.' His mother would murmur, passing again on her way to or from some endless chore, touching her husband again as she walked behind him, listening to the telling.

'T'were the way out. That's all,' his father would say, 'but your mother, aye, she were that brave. No wringing of her hands or falling to screaming or weeping, but straight off she went to get the surgeon, found the sticks and cloths for binding and held the lad's shoulder's herself while the surgeon, he pulled on the leg to straighten the bone and bound all into a solid, unmovable lump. And when young James yelped a bit she said, all calm as you like, "Our Gran did this with 'an dog when he fell. The bone was pokin' up and she put it back and bound it. Dog had a limp but he was alive and could get around. You'll likely be tha' same." And then she said to me, "And thankee for bringin' him out, Mr. Rosemurgy. If'n I could ask thee to help get him home to our Mamm…?"

'I said I'd take care of that for her, and I did.' His Pa would smile in that special way he had for his Mamm, 'She stood there, her cap tied under her chin, her legs bound to keep the bits from her skin and her shoes all soaked by the water in the sheds and she smiled at me. So on Sunday I asked her to walk with me after Church – and she did. So that's how it happened. She's been a steady girl, my Mary. And she's still as pretty as when I used to look at her in church.' He would say as he pulled himself to his feet either to shoo him, with his brothers and sisters, to bed or to their dinner, 'and you'll mind her or I'll have something to say!'

Shrieking with pretend fear his audience would scamper to do whatever had been bidden. Solomon would hide a grin, nod at the memory and draw on his pipe. Aye, Pa had been a great one for telling tales and yarns. Then there'd been that fall, with so many killed and Pa one of the few to get out but they all knew he'd never work again.

So, as soon as his Pa could sit up by the fire, there'd been his Mamm, up at the dressing sheds and no-one to say her nay and there she'd stayed, being made up to bay cappen, supervising the younger girls, until the chance came to get a place as a cook in the count house, which earned her more and was easier, drier work. So with her bringing home her bit of money, and with the family to help they'd got by and she'd raised all her little ones to adulthood and kept her husband longer than most. Many, too many, miners died early, were old men at forty but his Dad, bent and painful though he was, he was cheerfully entering his sixtieth year.

'Saved his life, that fall, though may God rest those others.' She would say to him as he helped her tuck the old man into bed. So now it was Pa and Mamm, his wife Jane and little Solly and soon, God willing, another little one, but these cottages, with the new roofs of slate, with two upper rooms, a scullery and a room, with a true, good fireplace, they were warm and had room so, with luck Dad would live on, and Mamm, to enjoy the children.

And his Jane, she had been the one to say, when they got the cottage, that there was a place for his Mamm and Pa, and Jane who encouraged the flower growing, 'to give Pa something bright to look at.' Jane, who was even now, with his Mamm to help, bringing another child into the world. He thought about his Jane, a gentle smile lighting his face, then a long scream cut through the peaceful evening and Solomon bit the clay stem of his pipe clean through.

'Solomon? Solomon, get along and boil me some more water.' His mother called from the doorway, and Solomon leapt off the wall, thrusting his broken pipe into his pocket and all but setting his jacket alight as he ran back to heft and carry and then be banished – again – from his bedroom and his wife.

'Take young Solly out for a bit,' his mother ordered, and sit your Father by the wall, he likes to smell the flowers in the dusk and watch the evening coming on – but don't you go far, if'n it comes onto rain again you'll need to get him and his chair inside. And don't let him sit there in the dark, for he will if you don't fetch him. I'll make hot tea for us all in a bit. Jane will like that, and as like will need it!'

Upstairs there was another long groan, and his Mamm took to her heels with another armful of cloths, hurrying upwards, calling 'I'm on my way now…'

'…And that was my great aunt Elizabeth's entrance into the world,' Solly told Timo, 'now, don't you think we'd better make a move? We can just, I think, squeeze out under the carriage if we dig a bit.'

'I'll dig, you tell me more about the Rosemurgys. About…your great grandfather was the one with the bad legs…so Solly would be your grandfather, little Solly your father?

'Aye.'

'Tell me more…,' Timo pleaded as he began scraping, digging in the soft stuff on the tunnel floor, making a gap between the rails and the carriage, wincing as his leg throbbed, his head swam and a pain gathered behind his eyes.

'I'll tell another, if'n you don't forget to dig.' Solly laughed, supported the other man's injured leg, contorted himself so he could dig too, and drew breath for another story.

'Solomon Rosemurgy, my great grandpa, he had a brother…'

*

…Solly was outside, bending from the waist and pouring water from a jug over his head, the dust in his hair turned to sludge before it sluiced out but now the water was running clean and he ran a hand back over his head, scooping the sleek black strands away from his face, blowing excess water from his lips and as he looked up, there was his Mamm, hurrying down towards him, her greyed hair loosening from its pins and bonnet, hands outstretched.

'Mamm?'

'Solly, Trevoole mine. A fall.' She gasped, 'A big one. Solly, your Uncle Weanie's down there. Him, at his age!'

Weanie, the youngest, weakest, sickliest of his Pa's brothers, had always been expected to die any day but had stubbornly defied all predictions and lived on to become a wiry, lean man with as much a skill for mining as his forebears and his larger siblings. Still, although he was only a few years older than Solly himself, the Rosemurgys as a family stubbornly thought of him as an old man, one likely to die any minute.

Weanie had been haunted by this expectation of immediate death all his life. Now, this day, they might all have been right and he may well have met the Reaper.

'Come on Mamm.'

'I'm going up there.'

'Of course you are. We all are.'

At the gate Jane, pale but stern had a subdued Solly and a tearful Elizabeth at her side, little Sophie, their third child, was in her arms. She had a knotted shawl in her hand.

'Ten this, it's supper.'

Solomon took the bundle. Ah, she thought of everything, did Jane. He felt two stone bottles, pasties, and by the heat, baked potatoes. He nodded at her and guided his small party out and up the ridge. Around them others were making their way to bal Trevoole, those with relatives working there who could be among those trapped, injured or digging through the rock to the rescue of their friends.

The mine was a-buzz with activity; Solomon took a draught from one of the bottles from Jane's bundle, took a pasty and went off to join the rescue parties. Mary worried that her son had already done twelve hours down a shaft, and prayed he would bring her brother out alive.

'We're going to see Uncle Weanie again, I know we will.' Elizabeth told Solly, who sat with her on the gorse-covered slope where the families had gathered, held his hand and wiped his nose when he didn't realise his tears and his snot were mixing on his chin.

Beside him sat his Gran, and his Mamm, while his Pa was off to find the trapped and injured. Solly felt pride in him like a bubble until he heard a child behind him saying the thing they all feared to think of the most.

'Aye, my Pa and my brother's down there,' he chirped in his high, innocent voice. 'They'll be either squished with their insides leakin' out or squeakin' and squakin' on breathing bad air. Ow…'

His Mamm boxed his ear 'Shush your chattering, Izz.

No-one wants to hear your nonsense.' She scolded, shaking an apologetic head at those around her.

Young Solly thought of his Pa, choking in the dark, like he himself had done last winter, when he had the croup. Then his Mamm had sat with him by the fire, wrapping warm flannel round his throat and making him breathe the steam from the kettle. He had been scared but there had been the candle, his Mamm's lap and his Pa holding him, and his Gran giving him the bad tasting stuff in the glass that made him so sick, and her holding him and saying, over and over, 'there little lamb, there. Gran's sorry, but it's to make you better. There now, my lamb.' And he had known he was safe.

His lip trembled and he prayed those men in the mine had a light, and hands holding onto them.

Jane, feeding Sophie, looked at her children, subdued and frightened by the tense atmosphere, the tears of adults, the waiting in the dark on this slope and not, as by now they should be, safe in their beds, and her heart sank.

She hoped to persuade them to the land, or a factory, or the railway - anywhere but the bal. But the copper was in their blood as it was in hers and there were few who would gainsay their heritage. She looked at Solly and saw, for a moment, the lad he would become, felt his fear as he put his feet on the rungs of the shaft ladder for the first time. Then there was her Elizabeth, who would be in the dressing sheds, or perhaps the count sheds if she was lucky – and Sophie, would there still be a mine here in Crowan when she was old enough to work? Part of her wished not, hoped the rumour that the tin was running out was true – but if that happened, if there was no tin or copper, what would happen to the families who relied on the mine for work, for their housing, for their livelihood?

Jane bent to her bundle and broke a pasty to share with her mother-in-law.

'I can't eat, my dear.'

'Yes you can. We had no supper and I need you strong, Mamm. Eat.'

Mary, reluctantly, nibbled at the food and Jane watched over them all as her children fell asleep under her shawl and Mary ate. She sighed. All she could do was look after them now and let the future take care of itself.

The night seemed endless to those waiting for news but for those below ground, the night had no meaning at all. Teams were working at the face of the fall; men were coming up exhausted, fresh teams were going down, into the sulphurous heat where candles were of little use and where the noises – the creaks and groans of the stone, the faint murmurings as the ghosts of the long dead came for the dying – confused those listening for the calls of the living.

Then, as stones shifted, as men yelled, a voice from the dark said, calmly as if he was at a picnic

'A' yop one of ye's brought a bottle. There's men 'urr with a thirst the size o' Lunnon itself!'

The cheer went up, and Solomon peered through the dust

'Weanie? Be you?'

'Solly, lad? Aye, be me. Now, gi' a drink, and get us out. There's men hurt bad, some dead, but some still living unless we's all choked by the time ye stir yeselves.'

Weanie had dug and shifted and propped himself a small tunnel through the fall, and he stayed with it, his narrow, short and dangerous road to freedom, re-propping, feeling for weaknesses, until the last man was out and then, as the stones he had placed so precariously collapsed and rolled free, Weanie slid down the fall and sprinted out of the dust cloud to the relative safety of the ladders.

Solomon went behind him as he climbed, alert to any slip or stumble. His Mamm'd kill him if, with Weanie not buried or suffocated in the mine, he let him fall to his death from the ladders. His watchfulness was unnecessary, though, for it was the man ahead of Weanie who slipped, and Weanie who caught him, held him and carried him up on his shoulders.

Above them, the news had already reached the families who waited in silence for the survivors to appear until the first man staggered from the pit; the tension broke and women ran, faces painful in their eagerness, to see if their man was up, walking, alive.

Then, as a figure appeared, with another across his shoulders, Mary Rosemurgy leapt forward with the younger women whose men belonged to the mine.

'Weanie Rosemurgy, you'll kill yensel! You put that man down this instant!'

…Timo chuckled,

'A fearsome woman, your great grandmother, by the sound of her.'

'Indeed. Tell me about your family, did you have a fearsome grandmother?'

'Oh yes. We are, now, as a family so respectable it hurts but only because a mere two generations ago my grandfather was a brigand, one of the last, who preyed on those who lived and worked on the slopes and peaks. My grandmother never married him but she stayed loyal until the end and was shot at his side by the revenuers for her pains. They are never talked about, we have no tales although, I suppose, they must exist. My father's father used to tell him wild stories about ambushes and living in the mountains; he was proud of his mother's ability to kill a man with a knife or gun and disappear into thin air. She knew the slopes so well she could move almost like a ghost…but my father has chosen not to remember. Ah, there's air, a space. We're at the other side. Can we get through?'

Solly explored.

'I believe we can, boy.' He clapped him gently on the shoulder. He had grown, Timo noticed, more Cornish.

'Underground, Solly,' he muttered, 'back to your roots.'

'I'm an engineer, not a miner. No mines left in Cornwall really. But I know enough to get us out, I reckon.'

Timo was barely conscious by the time Solly had freed them, dragging him under the listing coach. He was aware of being carried, slung across the Cornishman's shoulders, breathing in the smell of his scorched yellow jacket, the fumes in the tunnel, the smell of explosives. He was aware of being placed gently on the ground and hearing the screech of damaged hinges, metal on metal. He was aware of a hand on his arm then the swift uplift as he was shouldered once more.

'I've fixed the air conditioners for this stretch – I don't know about behind us. It's all mashed in there, someone did that to make sure a lot of people died,' Solly coughed.

Timo raged silently. His voice, his tongue, everything needed for speech seemed to have given up on him. He turned his head with difficulty and looked into the tunnel.

'Dying. I'm dying,' he thought, and felt tears leak from his eyes at the thought of the tolls for his loss that would be sung by the new bells, bells too young to yet be steeped in legends and traditions, and not the old bell he had known all his life.

He could see the outline of a tube ahead, with tubes and tubes and intersections, a whole web of tubes, tiny capillaries connected to everyone, everywhere, every time – the trick was to move through these tiny tunnels, these minuscule tubes, and if he could just reach, make himself absorbable…but someone was talking, someone he must answer.

'My son? Come, you can hear me? Agh, such a fool you have for a father, such a fool whose words inflamed those young hotheads to blow the tunnel at its inauguration, though I never meant that, never said that. How could they think that to kill as many as possible, to bring down the structure, was the way to keep our country pure and safe? It is my fault, and now my punishment is to lose my son. Maybe. But I won't let you go. If that man, that Britisher, can risk his life for you then I can give mine if I must.'

'Cornishman. He's a Cornishman. And I'd rather you kept your life, father. I think you're still using it.'

Timo opened his eyes, tried to hold out his hand to his father but had to wait for the older man to grip his fingers; his own arm, it seemed, was held still, a tube running from a bag of fluid at his side into the back of his hand.

'Tubes,' he murmured,

'It's to keep you hydrated…just you keep it there my boy. No fiddling.'

'No Father. '

'You owe your life to strangers, but they are not strangers anymore. These people. I spoke to them, I thanked them. Many of them have been here to the hospital to see you. They brought fruit and flowers, books and newspapers for you and sat talking, as I have done, to wake you up. They like you.'

Timo smiled, his father sounded surprised, bewildered by this fact

'And they brought me coffee, food, they found me an extra blanket for the nights,' his father added.

'You've been here all night?'

'All seven nights.' The older man was gentle now, 'we thought we would lose you. You have always been the rebel, the thorn in my side, but I would not lose you. Especially now when you and your friends and your tunnel have shown me something new, and even though it is new, I like it. You have shown me there is friendship to be found in unexpected places.'

'I'm glad…'

'And now I must go outside. The doctors wish to examine you.'

Timo saw two nurses and a tall man in a white coat at the door. He nodded.

'Just one thing, father. Tell me about our family. Tell me how we became who and what we are.'

Just for a moment his father stood rigid.

'There are new things in the past, Pa. As well as in the future,' he muttered. His father wavered, and smiled.

'Very well my boy. I will get myself coffee and when I come back, I will tell you how your great-grandmother walked over the mountains in winter to get medicine for her child, and how she stole the ruby from the mayoral chain. Perhaps, as we move into this new era, it is important to know and remember our roots. And don't call me Pa.'

Timo nodded on the pillow and submitted to the doctor's ministrations. By the door, Solly, with his black curls hidden by white bandaging, placed his gifts of newspaper and apples on a handy chair and grinned at the man who was one of the leading statesmen of his country and his day.

'Sir, I'm glad he's awake. To celebrate, will you let me buy you a pint?'

'No Solomon Rosemurgy, I will not. You may have saved my son, I expect you to let me buy you one!'

The two men left the room, already talking about the rebuilding of the tunnel, about the numbers dead and injured, about the punishments that should be given to the perpetrators, youths with no thought in their heads but to be heroes and who were now murderers; already friends and already listening to each other as well as talking while at the edge of town the multinational rescue teams, with the injured already in hospital or at first aid centres, began removing the bodies from the tunnel, and the town's foundry master began the task of rescuing the Old Bell.

Snowbloom

Slender stems

Leggy

Raising petals high above the ground

Which are unexpectedly called upon,

While snowbound

To act as umbrellas for delicate roots

Under frozen soil

A coil

Of silk-like threads

Holding the plant,

Satiating its appetite

Allowing life

To flow

To become a full-grown

Full blown

Snowbloom.

A QUIET LIFE

It was peaceful on the riverbank. Behind her the café buzzed quietly with muted conversation, the clink of spoons on cups, the warm aromas of toasted cheese and – she breathed deeply – bacon.

Mel turned her attention back to the river. Swans coasted elegantly by, ducking a graceful neck every so often to find a tasty morsel. In the bulrushes on the far bank she saw a flash of white and a coot scooted from one hiding place to the next, while a mallard upended in front of her. Mel chuckled.

"And to you." she thought, glancing at her phone, perched at the top of her bag for ease of access. It remained stubbornly silent but she saw the time. He was late. If he was going to be late, or couldn't find the place, he would ring. That was the deal.

She sighed. Maybe her daughter was right. Maybe Internet dating wasn't for her. After all, she had – during her dating site membership - met an aggressive on-line bully, two charming scammers, a handful of men inclined to be friendly but who hadn't lasted and now, this one. Michael. Who, it seemed, she was not going to meet at all.

He was a widower with two grown children, and had been working abroad, he said in his profile, but would soon be home and hoped to meet someone who could be a friend, maybe more, and share his long walks, sailing week-ends, trips to the theatre or a concert, or quiet evenings reading. She had contacted him. He had replied and they had talked for months via email and had even had a go at video calls but for some reason Michael's system had crashed each time he tried that so they had attached photographs by the handful and now – a meeting. He was flying – no, should have flown – into Heathrow that morning and it had been he who insisted they meet right away.

"I'll pick up my car and come to find you. I can't wait." He had said and Mel, somewhat dubiously, had agreed.

"I'll see you for lunch beside the river. I'm looking forward to it. But you seem, if you don't mind me saying, a bit reluctant."

"No. Not at all. No. Just don't want you to regret meeting because you're tired." She typed.

"I'll sleep on the plane and find you beside the river in time for a late-ish lunch." He had replied. "Believe in me, Mel."

But, it was past 2.00 pm. No phone call. No in person greeting.

"Guess he's a no show." She muttered, pulling one leg up so her foot rested on the front of the bench and wrapped her arms round it. She rested her forehead on her knee and closed her eyes.

"Stupid, stupid, stupid!" she mumbled, feeling tears beginning to heat up under her lids.

All kinds of things could have delayed him...but her phone remained quiet and memories of all the warnings about Internet scams, about catfishers, about emotional abuse whirled like an out-of-control merry-go-round through her mind.

And, there was the other thing...she had been as honest with him as with the other men who had liked her profile enough to suggest a meeting. One had chosen to go with another woman he had met who, he had told her cheerfully 'had a full set of mammaries and as he was a tit man, that was important.'

Mel had laughed and – unheard – called him a name. But wished him well. She was used to being mono-boobed, her cancer was long enough in the past to dull her sensitivities about her scar and prosthetic.

One man had fled after hearing she was not intending to be reconstructed. Another apologetically withdrew from what had seemed to be a burgeoning friendship saying his had lost his wife to that same disease and almost lost his mind.

"I just couldn't,' he said, 'go through that again."

Mel figured he may well have reasonable cause, and waved him off with only mild regret.

Then, she had met Michael and had begun to like him. Rather too much for someone she had never met face-to-face, she knew. And now, well, maybe they weren't fated to meet. Maybe he had decided against her lopsided self. Maybe she had been phished. She sighed.

If he had feet of clay, she thought, it was going to hurt. She really, really wanted him to be genuine.

The noises from the café changed. The smell of food faded. Now there were teacakes and scones and teapots and the clientele were fewer.

Maybe afternoon tea would save this outing from being a complete bust? No, she was not in the mood, in fact the thought of a teacake made her feel sick. Anyway if she opened her eyes she would find she was crying. It was ridiculous, at her age, to be this emotional over a failed meeting, over a man. But if she lost control of her breathing she would sob, she knew, so she breathed, squeezed her eyes shut and tried to take control of the hurt she felt, to re-direct it. She heard one of the swans hiss but didn't look up. Until a hand touched her shoulder.

"Mel?"

She looked up; saw white hair, dark eyes and a sheepish smile.

"Michael?"

The hand moved to her elbow to encourage her to stand but she was already on her feet.

"I'm sorry. I was late and when I tried to phone you there was no power and your number is in the thing. It seemed best to keep going and hope you waited for me."

"It's ok. I was watching the swans."

Michael looked down at the sunny smile, the traces of tears and brushed a thumb under her eye, gently. But all he said was

"We missed lunch, How about afternoon tea?"

Mel jammed her phone into her pocket and picked up her bag.

"Good idea. I was just thinking fondly of teacakes."

Cryogenics

Spring was dancing to its own heartbeat
Foot tappin'
Finger snappin'
Taproot bopping
Seed popping
Nothing in its seat
Beat.
But someone hated the music
Someone loathed the score
And quieted that syncopated heart
Froze the dancers to the floor.
The Winter's Queen just smiled
And said
'When my winter is through
The dance will be forgotten
And so, dear Spring, will you.'
But Spring was not forgotten
Her colours, scents and joys
Were kept alive in secret hearts,
Of tiny creatures,
Of little girls and boys.

Dreaming in the icy hedgerows
Or snuggled into beds
In warm pockets
Of fur
Of feather
Of hay
Or down
Or blankets
Curled,
With sunshine in their heads
They slept
Where the smallest creatures lived.

And then, one day, a song was heard
And trill of liquid notes
A lark that floats
So high
It broke the greyed out sky
Punching out an eye
And letting the sun shine through.
Spring woke from
Its cryogenic binding
Stretched out rootlings

Finding
The hiding
Birthings
And while the Sun burned
The Winter Queen to water
The dance resumed and rocked
Towards Summer
'Ya wanna dance to my
Foot tappin'
Finger snappin'
Taproot bopping
Seed popping
Nothing in its seat
Beat?'

Summer tilted it's sunhat
And joined the jive
Until bees buzzed in the hive
And lazy heat
Eased the beat
While the seasons swung
And flung
Joy
Into a quickstep

THE GARDEN

A black wrought iron gate leads from the rhododendron walk into the kitchen garden. The walls here are red brick and old but they keep the peaches and nectarines safe against them, and hold heat well after the sun goes down. There are, of course, no daffodils or tulips here, just regimented rows of vegetables with marigolds marching between the potatoes and round the tomatoes to keep black fly and aphids at bay. The only rebel is a large tub of Jerusalem artichokes, green foliage threatening to take over the space, heads nodding above the walls in season. He is a green and vibrant mutineer, but his tubers are so delicious that he is allowed to stay.

Neither the dogs nor I are allowed in the vegetable garden because we dig in all the wrong places, or so my husband says. But I think it's because that is his hideaway, that hidden garden, with his own greenhouse and a shed with a chair and a small electric ring where he heats soup and makes tea. He has one of those mini-fridges as well, to keep cold drinks cold when the sun gets hot

The cats are tolerated because you cannot tell a cat where not to go— they'll only ignore you —but the dogs just sit outside and whine while he's in there, hurt by their exclusion. I don't go in there at all now, and I am not hurt by my ex-clusion. He deserves his own domain.

I love this large, in part untamed, plot of ours. The vegetables, the lawns, the rose beds and the shrub edged walks, the stone terrace with its picnic tables, the fruit trees and the pond, even the utility area, with its washing line, dustbins, store for the mowers, and all the hid-den paths between.

But sometimes, you know, it changes. Not the seasonal changes, they are natural but the other, odd changes that I can't talk about because, well, people will think I am odd too.

Odder than usual, that is.

The thing is, there should be a path to one side of the vegetable garden, I mean, well, there is a path but sometimes it leads to the pond—we have one of those natural ponds where you can swim and have water lilies—and sometimes it leads to a summer house in another garden in another time.

In this other time, beside a little Hansel and Gretel house (not made of gingerbread but wood, with sweet scallop-edged shutters and a diamond-patterned door all painted the pink of seaside rock) is the old swing. It dangles, all old oak and grey, grubby rope, from the chestnut tree, and my sisters are there, watching me, waving to me. Sometimes, even when that other garden is invisible, I feel them, watching me across time, space and place when I am in my garden, calling to me to join them in theirs.

There they are still children playing at hide and seek, begging me, teasing me to find them and of course, I do. I always did.

It's magic, I think, because I've missed them so much and for so long. Or maybe this is a place where one of the holes in history lets the past bulge through. Perhaps they could tell me, but it's so good to see them I always forget to ask.

I was the youngest of them, the Forbes Girls as we were then; Lucy was the eldest, then there was Elizabeth, then Margaret and then me, Prudence, the baby at five years old. We loved to play on the swing there, and have tea in the summerhouse but best of all, in our childhood garden, was a good game of hide and seek. There were so many nooks and crannies, corners and secret places, it was a perfect place to hide, to be private, to do the things we were told not to do, like climb trees and crawl into the very heart of the bushes and stay, still as mice, while one of the grown-ups searched and called us for bedtime or for baths.

There was one place we were not allowed to go. At the far corner of the garden was a gate, a gate we were forbidden to use. It was usually kept locked but we had peeked through, of course, whenever the gardener left it open as he wheeled his barrow full of manure on its way to our roses, and we knew it led onto the lane which wound round to the farm.

Mr Burkiss, who had been a friend of our father's, lived there so we could not understand this curfew. Especially as the Burkiss family still came to our house for dinner or for drinks, so we told ourselves no-one would mind if we crossed the lane to the scrubby field opposite the gate where the village children used to play.

It was really part of the farm but it was tradition for the village school to use it for a sports field, and for football and cricket.

Everyone played there after school. But not us.

We never went there. We never went to school either. We had lessons at home and rarely went anywhere beyond the garden. Mother said we were all she had left, now the war had killed Daddy and we were never to leave her. So

Mother had a nurse and a companion and we had a governess and a tutor, and we had riding lessons, tennis and dance and we never went anywhere because all we wanted, all we had, was there in that house.

In that garden.

That's where we stayed, all high on the chalk lands of the North Downs, looking down at the Pilgrim's Way and the distant spire of Canterbury Cathedral, where Mother had met our father, where he admired her sketch of a window…

We never realised, then, how far Mother had retreated to the safety of the life she had known as a child. We never realised that Mother deliberately kept us inside and away from the village children. We just thought they didn't like us. We never realised she thought they were not our sort of people. We had no idea there were our sorts and their sorts. We had only the life we knew, though I suspect Lucy was beginning to ask questions for I had heard our governess say to her, more than once:

'Enough Miss Lucy. Your mother has her reasons for her decisions I am sure!'

It had silenced Lucy but I think, perhaps, she was feeling resentful, rebellious, in need of answers, of some kind of understanding of the reason behind the rule. It would explain why, that fateful afternoon, Lucy led us to the far corner, the forbidden corner, of the garden, lifted the latch on the gate and pulled it open. We all peeked outside at that prohibited world and thrilled at the possibilities of hedgerows, scrubby trees, muddy puddles and unexplored lands.

'An adventure,' said Lucy. 'I'm almost ten and I've never had an adventure. We should, you know, have them. Before we get too old.'

'Hide and Seek,' Margaret suggested. 'In the field. Before school ends and anyone sees us.'

'Mother's having her afternoon rest. She won't know. Think of all those new places to hide,' Elizabeth whispered.

'Can you be too old for an adventure?' I asked, remembering the grown ups whose pictures covered our piano top and who had gone away to war, never to return. It seemed to me that grown-ups had the biggest adventures of all.

But Lucy looked at me in her imperious way and shook her head.

'In all our books, adventures are had by children. Come on.'

So off they went, scampering across the lane in the sunshine, climbing through the hedge while I hesitated, a little unsure of this trespass. I heard a little scream

'I've torn my dress,' Elizabeth was saying.

'Come on Prudence!' Lucy shouted.

'Come on, Pru, there's nothing scary…' Margaret assured.

And then the earth and the hedge gave a huge roar and. sailed up into the blue sky. I went somersaulting over my head, landing on my bottom and flopping, rolling like a rag doll in the wind as the ground rocked and clods and bits of twig and leaves rained down about my ears, ears full of a kind of terrible, throbbing silence.

There was a soundless kind of plop at my feet and there was Lucy's arm, fingers crooked as though she was beckoning me. I knew it was hers, because on her wrist was the little silver bracelet engraved with the words 'Lucy, with love from Mummy. Christmas 1947' that Mother had bought her

Elizabeth had a gold one. Margaret had a little gold cross on a chain and I had a little silver cross. Just a few months ago we had opened and exclaimed and loved our presents together and had worn them ever since.

I wondered if Elizabeth's bracelet was still on her arm and tried to get up, to find out, to find my sisters in this chaos. And suddenly there was pain and there were people and crying, then dark rooms and Mother at my bedside praying and murmuring her thanks for the miracle of my survival and my body still being in one piece, and I never saw my sisters again.

Later, I learned that there had been an unexploded bomb. I learned that my sisters, in scrambling through the hedge just there had found it. I learned that no-one from the village went to that end of the field, keeping their games to the more level end closer to their own friendly community, avoiding our end in case they saw the mad woman (our mother, whose grief for our father had kept her both isolated and easily irritated) and anyway, the village people knew that Mr Burkiss buried sick cows at that end and no-one went there for fear of getting sick or turning into a werewolf.

I learned all that (though never how sick cows equated to werewolves, but it was a long held belief among the village children) from John Burkiss, whose father never forgave himself for not remembering the night in the war when a bomb came down. He knew it had landed somewhere in his fields just as he was getting in the cows, and that it never exploded, that it did no damage at all. But that night, in the rush of the milking, of his wife being in labour, of the daughter she gave birth to dying in her first hour of life, he had forgotten all about it.

Only our tragedy reminded him and from that day he lived with a guilt that was unreasonable in its intensity. I was sorry for him, but too involved with my own worries to do much but help him; instead I helped look after my mother who, once I was well again, became a complete recluse, an invalid, and a demanding companion.

I was twenty four years old in 1966, still shut away from a world full of change and excitement. My only contact was an illicit window, a television that had been bought by Mr. Burkiss, supposedly for the comfort of the string of nurses who came to look after my mother and left when she became too onerous. As she inevitably did. But he kept me supplied with a television listing magazine, bringing me a new one every week.

Thus I cheered as I saw England's football team win the World Cup, sang along with the Beatles, and heard about Martin Luther King Junior leading a civil rights march in Chicago and the angry white mob that attacked him. I loved it when Revolver was released in the UK and chuckled when John Lennon said the Beatles were more popular than Jesus and had to apologise. An avid watcher of the news I had opinions when Ronald Reagan, a republican and an actor, became Governor of California, cried when the Arno flooded Florence, and sighed over the idea of Truman Capote's Black and White Ball (the Ball of the Century) which was held in New York City on the 28th November. Which was the day my mother died, the day I was set free, the day John Burkiss asked me to marry him if, after two years of living without my burdens, I had learned to love him, if I chose him after tasting a normal life.

Such a sweet man, my John. I didn't need to learn to love him, I had done so all my life, but after those two years - which I spent in London experiencing the thing he called life - we wed, and are still together. We have lived, John and I; we travelled, had children, farmed and taught and throughout it all we have been, and still are, both best friends and lovers.

Oh, all these memories, flooding in from the past as I swim in our pond and look beyond the banks, hoping for that fuzz of light that heralded the arrival of our summerhouse, and my sisters.

The dogs are with me, here as I turn onto my back to float and look at the sky, Jack the Terrier has climbed out of the water and is chasing a bird while Rufus the Hound is dabbling with his paws at some unseen prey at the watery edge.

I hope it is not a frog. We do not encourage frogs for Rufus to eat them, and anyway they make him sick. I flip back to swim another width, putting my goggle-protected eyes into the water to see how the plants are doing and come up, blowing and pleased with the state of the pool. And there are my sisters, Elizabeth, Margaret, and Lucy all holding out their hands towards me. The dogs, I notice, have abandoned their prey and are sitting between the girls asking for, and getting, ear tickles.

Elizabeth, holding Rufus' long muzzle in her hands, looks up at me, smiling.

'Come with us, Pru. Please.'

Margaret helps me out of the pool, and as we run through the boundaries of space, time and realities I realise her hand seems warm against my chilled fingers and she holds them tight as we all run towards the summer house, arguing about who should be first on the swing. The dogs are barking in the distance and I think they are following, enjoying the chase. I hear my husband calling 'Pru, Pru!' and think he can see me running and will run after me.

'Pru shall go first,' decides Elizabeth, 'as it's been so long since we were all together.'

They clap as I swing, Margaret and Elizabeth, Lucy, and Mummy and Daddy who are standing on the porch of the sugar painted summerhouse, with a tray of lemonade and cucumber sandwiches on the table at their side.

I swing higher. My feet, in my small brown sandals, seem to graze the top branches of the tree and I know I have left my dogs and my husband forever.

I am saddened by that but, oh; it is so lovely to be home.

WINDOWS

I dreamed of people. I could see them as if through windows, much like the women in certain areas of Amsterdam (pale veined legs or mottled flesh all on show with intent) but unlike them, no one here was trying to lure with allure.

Here there was no recognition of a presence, no vendor or vendee. Thus I could watch their small actions, snippets of their unselfconscious lives with no hint of deception and no need to negotiate a transaction.

Strangely I didn't want to know more about the rest of their living: the things I never saw left me incurious. Instead I was filled with an urgent desire to know what it was like to be them, performing those small actions I could see. In my dream.

In my dream, I struggled to reach them, each one, to be them, doing that one thing, to know what it was like to be them, doing that. To reach out and know not just how and what they felt, but to feel the entirety of them, sharing their essential one, their awareness of themselves, performing that act, being within that act, being part of that act.

And in my dream…

I did.

-0

1: THE MAN WHO SHAVES.

There is a man, outlined by the framed window-glass through which he is visible as he strips his striped cotton jacket from his torso. He does this every morning, with an economy and grace of movement that is beautiful, and unexpected

He bares his chest, bares his arms, stretches them high and sticks out his tongue, squints and pulls it back in, shutting it into the cavern of his mouth as he squirts lather from a can and sculpts with it a beard of Santa whiteness. He wields a safety razor, one way and then another, the blade dancing across his face encased in its protective wire cage yet still cutting its dangerous path through his foaming art.

Pathways, labyrinthine and intriguing, appear across his large, bristle-beard darkened cheeks. They grow and widen, meeting when skin is clear of foam. He will never look apple-white, cleanly barbered and hot towelled. His jaw is too dark: too many years of shaving and the pourings of testosterone have given him a dirty blue tinge.

He is a man big of body, his skin loose and his muscles spent now from years of watching life, drinking life, of eating to comfort loneliness, hide disappointment and replace the thrill of being young, and dangerous, and fighting fit. His hair is slightly greasy, grey and a little shaggy, long but not unkempt. His pits are still dark but his chest is a mat of grey fluffy curls. What must it feel like, to be him, shaving?

I watch. Nose against the glass, feeling the hard, cold refusal of it against my skin, peering through, seeing my breath huff into droplets and feeling them run against my lips.... I am inside. Feeling the soap soft against me, inhaling the salty tang of unwashed crevices after a night's slumber. He/I prefers to shave before showering, or the mirror fogs up. We are peering into the glass now, seeing the light bulb - softened by a small pink shade - behind us, reflected in the mirror as if it was also ahead.
A past and future light.
The water runs against my lips as I cup a hand, a large, coarse hand, to rinse the foam from my left eye.
Careless.
I am he and he is me and - it smarts.
But now the razor moves, dances, stripes delicately down with little sound. The follicles bristle but they give up small lengths of them-

selves, sacrificed to the blade, the strength, the god of the fatal dance.

The joy of moving this instrument across and through my face is intense and yet, behind my joy he is merely mechanical. So many times has this hand performed this action that it does not need guidance. So many times has he stood here, this man, behind the face being shaved by the hand, which seems now almost disembodied.

He thrills to the taming of his beard, though; as more stubble is rinsed from the blade into the scummy water, with a thrill that is, itself, a pathway. A pathway back to boyhood when he idolised his father, when the ritual of passing from man to boy, the first shave, was still ahead of him. When he watched his father mix lather in a mug made for the purpose and apply, with a bristled round-headed brush, this mixture to his face.

Sometimes he would stand at his father's' side, perched on a chair, and pull shaving faces into the mirror. He made his father laugh and, unsteady of hand, he would pull the blade away from his throat and dab white lather onto the boys' nose. The boy/man would squeal and flee, returning to have the offending blob shaved away with the blunt handle of the razor. Now the boy and man are within a membrane's width, a moment of reality away from each other and in the pathways lays the route to their meeting.

Left cheek, upsweep twice, sidesweep, wash the blade.

Engrossed in this ritual he is unaware of the thrill he feels, or the moment of almost stepping into a time gone or even the slight melancholy that goes with his father's' memory. Instead he thinks

"I must pick up my suit from the cleaners and collect the wedding present."

Tomorrow his niece will marry and he has bought a nice stainless steel electric kettle to give as bride price, and as bribe.

He had thought she and the boy would never get around to it.

The water is cool now, and the foam, clogged with dark grey bristle, floats like tainted icing on the top.

Pull the plug and watch it swirl.

Is it on, or across, the equator that it swirls the other way? If this reversed would it take more of the scum, or still leave globs deposited on the shiny white ceramic of the sink?

The water from the tap gushes, it is hot on his fingers as he swishes it across the soap. His wife hates to face a dirty sink.

Cold water, sloshed over the skin and torso, droplets clinging to the hair, towel the eyes clear and dab the face, peering into the slightly blurred glass of the mirror, feel satisfaction at a good shave, a slight eternal disappointment at not finding himself apple-white, shiny clean and distinguished.

Gasping from the cold shock he turns to the shower. His fingers grasp the cold metal of the controls, water gushes, cold first then steamy but it is the cold I feel

The I, not the me/he of my brief stay within his skin and

In my dream

there is the taste of the water on my lips, the cool glass beneath my searching fingers and I am outside again.

It is raining.

I am drinking the rain and wondering why, if I was he, there was no sense of his awareness of himself, only of the physicality of his living. Did I miss it? Was I so enthralled with this new physicality that I failed to find the Self?

Why do I remember his father but know nothing of this man's' essence when he and I were, briefly, a new Me/He?

Is he as apart from himself as I am apart from him? Is isolation all there is, all that remains? Even from Oneself?

I drink the rain, and like Alice, lose myself in another world.

-0

2:. THE NEW MOTHER

My dream here is different. I am part of her dream, I am the face, the voice, the person she searches for in order to say to someone the things she really feels.

She is outwardly one thing, the happy young mother with a loving young husband and a beautiful baby. Her home is comfortable, although the budget is strained, but her friends and family support her, help her, buy things for the baby and treats for her. She hoards these for she knows this generosity will not last but is grateful now and pleased by this care. She smiles and is happy inhabiting this place.

But on my arrival, I find there is no her/me combination, only me inside a vast and bleak emptiness. I cannot find her to complete the synergy of her/me. Inside there is no reflection of her, or her happiness.

There is a completely different landscape.

She is tired.

She is bone-weary.

She is absent.

She cooks and cleans with teeth-tingling-stomach-flipping revulsion as her fingers touch the residues of old food, greasy dishes and gritty cleaning products - always the cheapest, she cannot afford brand names, and isn't sure of their value, even if she could.

After the cleaning, she bathes her child and marvels at the smooth skin, at the laughter and the splashing and softness of the baby bath bubbles.

These she will afford.

She enjoys these games, treasures them and tucks the memory of them away like jewels, to be gloated over later when the giver has left her alone. But there is nothing of her own desires, her own feelings, her own fears. She enjoys her child, but as I do when I watch them through a barrier, a pane of glass.

Where is she? I cannot know for I cannot share her actions. Much as she loves, much as she concentrates on the temperature of the water, taken with such care and efficiency through a cocked elbow, she has hidden herself. In my dream I am here, inside, standing in this bleak and empty landscape alone, compelled to search - but where? Is this person, this woman, this fascination to be but a facsimile of the true life? Is this what I must learn?

Or is there, somewhere, the small lonely voice of the child this woman once was, cowering in the dark, afraid of the adulthood, the parenthood at the door? Is there the girl who was a child, a daughter, a sister, a lover, in here somewhere in this wilderness? If so how do I find her? In my dream, it is thus: I sit in this dusty inner self until there appears on the far horizon, a child, a barefoot and ragged child. She is neglected because her body is now adult and must pretend to be part of the adult world yet it is she who plays with the baby, forging the jewels the mother will garner. Of course. She and I share games until she remembers how to be a child, until she knows that it is the fate of all children to wait until adulthood before their true enjoyment of childish things may begin.

She laughs and the sun shines.

She cries and daisies flower in a grass that grew, unnoticed, as we played. In my dream, I do not know why the she/I happened only in this way and why I could not share her motherhood.

I do not know why the gentleness and delight in her relationship with her baby that was visible through that tiny window, the one on the side of the black-haired woman which was not that of the shaving man, was denied my synthesis.

In my dream, I do not know.

Awake, I am both curious and mystified.

And I still do not know what it is like to be part of such a union, to hold such a small, soft, wriggly life - a life borne within, given to the world through a doorway of pain and forever bonded as flesh of my flesh - and to splash water over its tiny crown, protecting its eyes so carefully with my hand and delighting in the tiniest smile, the softest gurgle.

Why? Will I know, one day? Either in my dreams or here, in this world, behind my own pane?

-0-

There was a child who, behind a window about three floors above the shaving man, was in the habit - in my dream - of getting out of bed on clear nights and looking up at the stars.

I wondered what she saw that gave her that ethereal air of fear and fascination and took, when not dreaming, to studying the clear night skies myself.

There came a night when the dream overcame my interest in the Great Bear, and my idle curiosity in the craters of the moon, one of which - as I sat staring up at the lunar fullness - swallowed me with a crater that had become a mouth. It was a dream, an ordinary dream, there was no window for me to peer through and yet, suddenly, she/I were crouching on her window seat, a padded, comfortable thing, not like the hard, varnished wooden lid of my own toy box-cum-seat and she/I shared a true epiphany.

In the drawing of that breath time froze, became a moment out of time, maybe a moment when Death hovered, pausing to greet or identify or warn as he passed either her, me, or the she/me entity.

I remember the chill of his passing. I remember the stars. And I fear that somehow, they remember me.

I remember the she/me entity flying into a spangled eternity, excited by the weightless freedom of non-physical being although aware still of the sense of body, the strong sense of self.

Around us, voices spoke from the emptiness.

'Go back/'

'You have so much yet to experience/'

'Love/'

'Childbirth/'

'Motherhood/'

Of course she/I, lost in our own exhilaration, uncaring of these things, kicked out, swimming free in the seas of space, surfing the firmament. Now, I know. And I care. I hope she does. Then, youthful and heedless, I/she felt our weightless speed and gloried in it.

'Don't go any further/'

'Don't go/'

And a single voice.

'You'll lose yourself. You won't be you. You won't be able to go back.'

She/I hesitated on the crest of some huge and pulsing cosmic wave and felt, in that moment, a sense of unravelling, of non-being, of parting with the sense of ourselves, the self she knew as herself and I knew as me – had always known as me. We parted there in the firmament and what she felt can only be a guess but for me, crowding in, came thoughts of physical pleasures; the sensual thrills of touch, taste, smell, sound. There came memories of warm sun on my skin, a hand on mine, sand under bare feet, the smell of the woods after rain, all washed over me, leaving me feeling abandoned at the idea of their loss. Awareness of plays not seen, books not read, music not heard, places not visited, people still to meet, things to see and do drowned me.

Panic flowed through my transparent veins and my scream came from an invisible throat and with a gut-roiling wrench and a physical thump that jarred my bones I was in my bed. My night-light was on and Jack and Jill, visible in its glow, were toiling endlessly across the pink field of my wallpaper.

My screams were now audible and physical tears were wet on my cheeks. My parents came running in, scooped me up, soothed and patted. My father brought hot, sweet milk, which I always hated but he meant well and I wanted them to stay so I drank it, still hiccupping sobs and shaking. Outside I was warm and cosseted but inside was still the cold of eternity and the loneliness of losing my inner self. There was an awareness of non-physicality. I kept repeating

'I don't want to die. I don't want to die.'

'Perhaps you won't' said my mother, tucking me in again and picking the cup delicately from my fingers. 'Perhaps by the time you've grown up scientists will have discovered a way to stop us all dying.'

That was the moment I knew my mother and father feared the same thing, and wanted so badly to say, 'I know. It's not being. It's being part of something else, something that isn't just you. And not knowing where all the things you learned and loved are when you're not you.......!'

But the words failed to come and as they left me, my mother and father, my father said 'What was all that?'

and my mother replied 'Just a nightmare.'

I wanted to shout, 'No!' to holler, to break things. There was this huge something, this frightening emptiness and its Guardians, a place where freedom seemed total until it swallowed you whole! It was not a nightmare. There should be discussion! Sharing!

But they had already gone back to bed, sleep was pulling me in and anyway I was aware that somehow there were not the words in my vocabulary, perhaps in any language or vocabulary, to convey the cold beauty, the freedom, exhilaration, panic, the sense of un-being, undoing, unbecoming yourself. The emotion was too dense, too intense to describe properly.

I fell asleep and in the morning knew it all to be impossible to broach, partly because my primary recollection was the fear. It's a fear that has

lingered throughout my life and which I find difficult to externalise, or explain. Back then, when I woke and remembered, I clung to the idea of science saving me to hold back the screaming.

I was three years old, and I never looked at that window again, or gave the stars more than a snatched, frightened glance as I quaked, frozen in memory, at their cold beauty.

FAMILY TRAITS

My father was sitting in his favourite chair in his favourite room in the house – the library. It was a big room, lined with oak shelving that was crammed with books, all kinds on all subjects – paperbacks, hardbacks in all types of bindings. This was not a library bought by the yard.

The windows were tall, inset, with chairs tucked into the space so one could sit and read by the last of the daylight, the floor was wood, with old but well kept Persian rugs, small dark wood tables and scattered armchairs. The scent of their polish added to the aroma of old paper and dust – it had always been my idea of an ideal room in a gentleman's club.

He sat, oxygen mask to hand – the cylinder tucked discreetly behind him - and a book on his lap.

'Hello Dad, what are you reading?'

He smiled and showed me. It was not a novel, as I'd thought, or a memoir or book of essays –

the book he showed me was an old photograph album, leather- bound, tooled and scuffed beautiful item. He handled it carefully, almost with reverence.

'See that blodge there? That was made by my grandfather's thumb. He always held this book the same way, this way.' He demonstrated, so his thumb fitted across the blodge and the spine of the book rested in his palm.

'I can see him now, holding it for me to see. I can see myself, sitting on his knee, listening to stories of all these dead relatives. Those stories and his interest gave me my love of history. Look, you can see how it's worn in to the shape of his hand.' He said.

I nodded, my throat tightening. His grandfather had been a large man, with big hands; my fa-ther – always smaller – had lost weight. He looked dry, papery, shrunken now, disappearing into the disease that was lurking in the dark places within him.

He opened the book to reveal photographs of people long gone, places long changed, days long past.

'There. That's your great-grandfather. His name was Albert. I was given my middle name in his honour; apparently he was a kind, good man. I've told you about him.'

I nodded again.

He had. Often. Anecdotes, family legends about Albert had abounded. My father seemed fascinated by this brilliant gentle giant whose talents had been the base from which the family firm had grown. Perhaps because my father was not known for kindness and goodness – he was a businessman, a wheeler-dealer, selfish, hard and ruthless in his youth and yet, he had loved me, had listened to my problems, helped me to grow, let me make my own choices - be they good or bad – and been there to help pick up the pieces.

He had not been at every sports day, every event throughout my childhood and youth but he'd always been there when it mattered.

His brother, my uncle Patrick, was the gentle soul of their generation who, I had been told, took after Albert. Like him he worked with his hands, loved and understood heavy machinery – envied even now Albert's lifelong involvement with steam engines of all kinds, with the railway – though Uncle Pat only got to play with locomotives at week-ends when he and various other enthusiasts got together to restore old trains. There are many home movies and DVDs showing him proudly pointing to bits of rusting metal, beaming and saying 'My Great-Grandfather built that! Isn't it wonderful?'

Meanwhile, my father would be off in a corner, shaking hands and talking to people who could help him grow the family firm, make him richer, more powerful, make the firm bigger, more respected, make it a corporation to be feared. He had made the family firm into a global concern, my father, and himself and the family richer than any generation before us. He was not a man people liked but he was respected and, for me, he had always been a good father, and I loved him.

And now I was losing him.

His thin, bloodless finger pointed, he held the book towards me – with some difficulty - so I could see the photograph. I leaned in to look and smelled the musty smell of his illness as I looked at a strong man of large frame, smiling at the camera. A black and white snap it nevertheless showed Albert as a happy man, smeared in oil, his overalls filthy, standing in the sunlight looking away to one side, his expression one of a man taking time away from his pleasures in order to please someone else. His colouring, I thought, would be like

Patrick's – reddish brown hair, dark eyes and white teeth in a tanned face.

'He looks like Pat.' I said. 'Or rather, Pat looks like him.'

My father nodded.

'He, Albert, and his brother – Andrew, they began the firm you know…well, of course you do. Albert's engineering genius, Andrew's business flair. Brothers…build and destroy, build and destroy…'

His voice grew fainter, his thin, boneless body relaxed back into his chair and he slipped into one of the increasingly frequent dozes he took during the day. I caught the album as it slipped from his lap, closed it carefully and was putting it on the table at his side when a thin wad of paper fell out. Picking it up, I saw my father's eyes flicker open and stood, like a school boy caught raiding the sweets jar, with the folded papers in my hand.

'Ah – good' he murmured, 'I wanted to show you that. Read it, boy.'

He gestured to a leather easy chair beside the window. I walked to it. If he wanted me to sit there and read this old letter, then that's what I would do. I saw his lips pull into that satisfied half-smile he gave when people did things they way he wanted them done.

I sat, unfolded the papers and looked at the handful of pages covered in beautiful cursive script.

'These were written by Albert!' I said, startled into speech. A gentle, feather-light snore was my only reply.

So, I began to read. It was not a letter, pre-cisely, but an account of something that had happened, something that clearly disturbed him

'My name is Albert Singleton, of Singleton Brothers. I write to clear my mind,' he began, 'to set down the things that happened so they are no longer haunting my psyche and so that others, in the future when perhaps it will no longer matter, will know what I saw, what I believe to be the truth of what happened that day. Our town is growing quickly and there are places where the municipality meets the country that are more industrial yards now, than anything else. The railway repair yards and terminals are in just such a place, although there are still some scrubby fields where children play and people walk – there are plans for them to become parks - but they are, on the whole, more urban than rural in nature.

On this day, cold and frosty but bright, as I was waiting for the 9.30 to pull in – she had a problem that needed fixing – I saw a woman I recognised. Her name was Mary Weatherby, she was a Nanny and was taking two children, a baby in a pram and a small girl, for air and exercise as she did most days. Though usually she did not have the two together. The little girl needed a lot of attention and on this day she was playing up, running, always just too far ahead for safety or comfort. I could hear her high little voice calling,

'Chase me, Nanny. Chase me!'

Nanny Weatherby pushed the pram along the packed cinder path, following its serpentine trail through the fields. I knew she, and the baby's nurse, often came there where it was away from the streets, but not too far, where the child could run and yet where the perambulator rolled easily and they were not too far from their tea, the house being no more than three streets from the one time countryside.

'Come on, Nanny. Chase me! Chase me, Nanny.'

Nanny stopped, shook her head, sighed a bit too, I would think. Her charge looked such little lady in her wine coloured velvet coat, with its matching, boat shaped hat and tiny kid gloves, the whole outfit a miniature model of her mother's, made because she had adored it and the dressmaker thought she was a sweet child.

The sweet child had now, in my view, the wind under her tail and the devil in her heart as she twisted and turned ahead of the pram, taunting and demanding.

I could, in my mind, already hear the sad, winsome tones as she said,

'It was a lovely walk, Mummy. It's a shame Nanny won't play, or do bird calls…but it was still a lovely walk.'

How would I know this? The children were my niece and nephew, my brother's children, heirs to Singletons and the bane of Nanny's life, I thought.

Nanny began to trot, no doubt hoping the baby would sleep through it all

'Come on, Nanny.'

The child spun on her toes, impatiently.

'Come on, Nanny. You are never much good at running games, but now with Baby you are all clumpy and slow. Silly Nurse, having a cold when I want to run.' She called.

I blushed as I stood on the terminal platform and wanted to go up to Nanny Weatherby and apologise for my niece's behaviour.

Then, little white legs twinkling, shoes crunching on the white, frost-rimed cinders, the child took off, quicksilver flying through the cold air. Cinder chunks spattered as her feet pounded, swinging her body back to slide to a halt, blocking Nanny's somewhat rheumaticky progress as she suggested their game would be so much better if the pram could be put aside for a while.

Nanny's thin shoulders tipped forward, her beaky face thrust downward, balanced on her stringy neck.

'Leave Baby alone so I can run round with you? The idea!'

'I hate you!' The words were screamed, break-
ing the cold air into splinters.

The child spun on her heel and was speeding
away, across the open space, kicking frosted
snowdrops with vicious strikes that broke her
stride. But she was fast.

Too fast for the Nanny, with or without the
pram.

'You little demon! You come here.'

I heard it in her voice, shrill and thin, that she
knew this charge of hers was beyond her skills,
and in that moment knew that the child knew
it, too. Nanny threw her slight weight against
the good quality tank of a pram and forced it,
as well as her shaking legs, up the incline
where a velvet coat hid in the bare twigged
bushes.

'Don't you go across onto the tracks,' she
called, knowing, I thought, that she was doing
it all wrong while her fright prevented her from

trying a smiling, smooth tone, a hug, a game. The velvet coat burst from bushes, the high-pitched formless laughter trailed back in the wind and the child was on the tracks, performing an approximation of the Scottish sword dance between the sleepers.

Nanny saw the plume of steam belching around the curve, she heard the child's laughter, the 'can't catch me' ringing above the whistle. Nanny turned the pram sideways against the low slope, fastened the brake, left her bag under Baby's blanket, and ran.

She threw herself forward, reaching desperately ahead. The steam huffed, the scream of metal on metal, the heat that enshrouded her as her fingertips grazed the little wine coloured velvet coat. All her strength was in that one last push as the train wheels rolled over her body and the noise of it drowned the child's screams and then there was nothing but silence. Briefly.

Before panic and pandemonium ruptured the scene.

The child was enveloped in a man's arms, her face pushed against a rough jacket. People whispered, cried, sobbed, vomited. Someone picked up Nanny's hat, catching it as it bowled merrily off the tracks. There was a shoe beside the line, still encasing a slim foot, the ankle bone of which rested against the rail.

It began to snow, lightly, a damp white drizzle that made people shiver even more. Against the skyline, the pram stood, monumentally lonely —the baby's cries were lost in the screams and hubbub of the people, the huffing breath of the train.

Luckily, someone saw and rescued and, recognising me, brought the pram to me, the man who had pulled my niece away handed me the crying girl with some relief.

'Go to your Uncle, pet. He'll look after you.'

'Tragedy.'

'Terrible.'

'Take the children home, Albert.'

There was a restive shift, a move to get things cleared away. After all, the train, paused and stationary could hardly stay where it was, on the line. And people had places to go to, other people to meet. The railway men had wives who would be complaining about spoiled meals if this detritus of death lingered too long. Someone jumped on a bicycle and set off to find a policeman. Nanny's demise, the tear-sodden child, and the baby—it was for someone else to deal with, although, of course, it was a terrible, terrible thing to happen.

I took the children home.

There was, there had to be, an inquest. Nanny was a hero, her death a misadventure, for had she not pushed that poor little girl clear of the train? Not – quite.

'I don't know.' I said to my wife once the inquest and the funeral, both of which I attended, were over.

'I thought the little one jumped back by herself, off the track, just as the train hit – she wanted Nanny to – she lured her in front of the train and then jumped back. Made the poor woman stretch out – wouldn't have had a chance. I thought she did it on purpose. Born in the shadow of Hell, that one, I've often thought and though I don't want to believe it...'

'Then don't, Albert.' My wife said. 'She's your brother's child. You can't say anything – how could you and he work together if you did and you're doing so well. Anyway it couldn't be that way, you must have been mistaken. They said the Nanny saved the child's life at the cost of her own.'

I let her calm me, fell quiet, and have stayed so for years. I couldn't take away the poor dead woman's bravery, and anyway, who would believe me if I spoke against a child like that? But every night, even now, I still dream of my little niece on that day, of the face I saw as she surveyed the human wreckage under the wheels; I am sure that, just fleetingly, she smiled, a sly, triumphant twist of the lips, before her mouth opened and the screaming began....

'Alicia Singleton, my great aunt' my father murmured on waking. His crackle-leaf voice made me start, I'd been sitting, staring out of the window at the wide sweep of the lawns where I had played as a child, thinking about Albert and how he would, if he had been anything like Pat and I felt he had been, suffered under his suspicions. He would have hated himself for thinking such things but been haunted by the vision of that little, sly face above the mangled remains of her Nanny, made wretched by his need for justice and the need for compassion, and by his fear both of, and for, the child Alicia.

'I'm sure Albert was right, said my father, more strongly now, ringing his bell, asking for tea and perhaps a plate of crumpets and of course his son would be joining him.

'Hell of a story, Dad.' I said, rising, folding the papers, walking over to give them to him to re-place in the book.

He shrugged

'There are lots of other stories like that. People get fucked up.'

He handed me the book, waved at the papers. 'Keep them, boy. Yours now. But – care for them. Don't forget the past. It's your past, after all. Your roots.'

I wasn't sure I wanted to think too deeply about that, so I nodded, thanked him and changed the subject. Over tea and crumpets we talked about horse racing, cars, about his dogs and the care of roses.

Three days later he died in his sleep. Six days later I received a letter from him, with a manuscript.

'My life,' he wrote, was always complicated. There have been deaths – Albert was right about Alicia – it is a family curse, perhaps, the lack of humanity in some of us, the overcompensation in others. I killed six people in my life – your mother being one, because I thought she was going to leave me. I regretted that. The others were business competitors. Be aware, my son, beware of yourself.'

'Bit late, Dad,' I thought, as I put my signature on the contract that sold my shares in the firm and looked forward to a life of sun, fun and glamorous women. And money.

Lots, and lots of money.

THE WEB WE WEAVE

There was a woman on the train. She had with her one small suitcase, a large handbag or briefcase and a brown box slightly larger than a shoebox, tied with string. The suitcase was well used, but not battered. The box was old but sturdy and the woman, not very tall but slim and dressed in a black suit, could have been travelling to, or from, a funeral or perhaps a business meeting. She was pretty, in a formal way, but she looked tired and sad, and the droop of her mouth softened her face so, strangely, her sadness increased her prettiness. At first, as the train wound through the coun-tryside, she sat with her head against the back of the seat. Her face impassive, no one could know what she was thinking, or what she felt.

She had, over the past weeks, sat with her fa-ther holding tightly to his hand, anchoring him to the world, comforting him with her presence. She, his youngest child by many years, his well-beloved as he called her, had been there as he took his last breath, had kissed his cheek, had cried so many tears as she arranged his funeral. Then, alone, she had taken the train to the town where the University, and his rooms, still guarded the secrets of his other life, his scholarly life, not the one they shared in the village, where he was important merely as her father.

There was little she wanted to keep. His desk and chair would be hers and were even now on their way to her cottage, to the room that was her study. His books she had boxed, after offering choices to his students, his colleagues, his friends, and sent them home too, adding as an afterthought his notebooks and letters. She had handed out bequests according to the instructions in his will, sent his clothes to a charity shop, thrown out a few bits though he had been a tidy man and collected very little rubbish, very few mementoes. But, in cleaning out his room she had discovered a man she had not known. She had guessed at his existence, of course, but never met him; now she found evidence of a woman he had loved, people he knew, shows he had seen and holidays he had taken without her, without her knowledge. She visited the woman, gave to her photographs that showed her and her lover together, happy, content. She gave, too, of her time as she drank whisky with her and listened to anecdotes, reminiscences, handed a tissue to mop unexpected tears. She gave her address and her phone number did his daughter to this woman who had been his love. Tears were shed in unison, then together, hugs were exchanged, and the daughter understood why her father had loved, here, after her own mother had left.

She thought, as she sat on the train, that she had found an unexpectedly close, warm link to her father in that small, cosy little house in the town, not far from his now ex-rooms.

And, she had found her brother. Here, in this box.

She remembered nothing about him, her brother. He had been much older than her and used to being an only child when she was born. He blamed his mother's desertion on his father and her own birth, remembering how she – his mother - had begged for the abortion she never got, remembering how she had birthed and fled. Her brother blamed her father, but not her, not her infant self. She was innocent, he said. She had never asked to be conceived, or to be born. But still he ignored her. He had never contacted her and had never spoken to his father from the day he graduated, the day he left home, the country, and their lives, until the present. He had never acknowledged their father's illness, death, funeral, anything. Her father, over the years, had ceased to speak of him.

She thought he had decided to forget.

And then, in a box, this box, at the back of his cupboard, she found a handful of photographs of his son in various stages of his life, often with his father, pictured laughing together. Two of the pictures – the graduation and the newspaper publicity shot – were mounted in plain silver frames and with them, tucked under them, was the first draft of the boy's first book, with some newspaper cuttings and reviews. Her brother was famous now, a scholarly author in demand for television, radio and lectures. She had attended one once, and would like to have gone to him, to say how much she had enjoyed it, but he looked austere, his gaze cold, and she had been frightened to approach.

Now, in the train, she opened the box, untying the string carefully and precisely, lifting the photographs out with care and putting them aside in the box lid, weighting them with a lump of amber she took from her bag, a thing her father had used on his desk as a paperweight since he had been a student. Then she lifted the pages, tapped their edges into neatness and looked at the first page. Printed, but not a full draft of the whole book, this was the beginning, the time when the idea began to take shape – he had never realised, she supposed, that he had left it behind. Thinking he had cleared all trace of himself from the family home, he had overlooked this and it had been found by their father – perhaps as he packed the bedding, moved the furniture ready for removal? She knew he had sold that house, bought the cottage that was now hers, as a start for a new life, her life. But he had found, kept, and written on this first page. Sighing softly, thinking of his silent (to her, anyway) pain, she began to read.

**

IN THE BEGINNING, IS THE END

A Novel

First Draft.

By My Son. – I am So Proud of you...your loving father.

Through the something that has been wrapped about the body of the world in natal eons, holding and guiding it past infant growth, something stirs. There is a shiver of awareness, a noticing that flickers within the firmament. Ribbons of the ever-shifting universe are slipping, sliding, skimming and bringing, without intent or discernible consciousness, thought. There is a sentience, a sputter-gutter of that which will become me, but in that place that is no place, time that is no time, there is me that is not - yet - me.

In that place that was no place there were the first multiversal births, the parents bringing forth their children - the many Universes - and then those children bringing forth their own children. One of which is this world, this Child Orb that I bear and nurture but not-yet-me is a neglectful nursemaid and fails to notice the agonies of this child's metamorphosis. Until, that is, it begins to move differently, to hum among the spheres with a different tone, to throb with a different pulse. Only then, attention finally recalled to these duties from ponderous and unquantifiable, unrecognised philosophies it is to find this orb-child playing with the fabrics of celestial silvers, borrowing the celestial sounds.

The Orb is threading and weaving the stuff of place that is not yet place and making a solidity, creating oceans, bound to the Moon, its first creation, and filling this life with other, smaller, simpler and yet more complicated lives.

The Orb is, too, using time that is not time to produce a military, machine-like tick-tock of measurement, to have within its bounds a borrowed dimension of Time marching on tiny booted feet, ever onward.

Large mountains point up while their feet are bound in the rock and the earth. Air moves and sings, shouts and breathes like a lullaby. Creatures with a will that is not mine are moving and living, being nurtured by this child in my care. All this fills my eye.

My eye.

My eye on this child-world.

Mine.

And there, suddenly, was a tentative tendril of 'me'.

As with this child that I held while it grew, I transformed. In being aware of the child-world as a separate entity my being became aware of me.

And my 'I' turned my eye on this child-world with a new gift of vision. I saw movement and in becoming aware of movement I found the nature of it and so learned, clumsily at first, to use it. Carrying the orb, for it could not, yet, be abandoned, I progressed slowly through the ebbs and flows, moving, stretching, touching…. Finally I set the child-orb down in the comfortable place in which it had birthed, independent now of my warmth and protection, and looked with keen eye to see the creatures living such short but magnificent lives on its surface.

They thirsted, so it gave water, streams and rivers of fresh, cold, pure liquid. They hungered so it gave fruits, roots, and the means to kill for meat. Killing – where had this orb learned to kill? Exploding, dying stars…firmament that was no more became other matter, it said, so let living meat do the same.

Then the child danced, turning in the place where I had rested it, letting the warmth and light of the sun warm it, and its creatures, in turns. And thus the life upon it prospered. And I...I hungered to share that rich, chaotic, sensual, opulently tactile life. I craved, I longed, I wanted....and saw that, for the blink of time that was a lifespan for the creatures there, I too could taste this physicality, this living.

There is one moment when I hear one beat Then more fills the air, the ground. There are echoes through my blood, my skin, my bare feet, the thrumming, humming drumming of the beat. Above and below, inside and outside the beat there are complex contrapuntal motions creating rhythms. Notes beat to the scent of harmony. Cowering and leaping into discordant passion, the slower, soothing congruence of gentler melodies envelops, enwraps, holds, tortures, pleasures, and enchants the Body Audience.

Music. Some is in the womb of a concert hall where orchestras play and their sounds are flown on the ether from wave to wave so we can, in isolation, hear and hum. But most is outside the hall, where birds serenade the dawn, where there are shouts, laughter, cries, where things rattle and roar, where the sea laps, swooshes, crashes, rain patters, clatters, lashes and wind hums, rustles, wails or screams. Where cars thrum, snarl or hoot. Where there are thunder rolls, baking rolls, pops and booms. Where there is growling, snarling, bellowing, bawling, hollering, yelling, whispering, lullaby hums, gentle murmurs, loving mutters in all keys and volumes, all echoing. All carried in the air in plumes and skeins and bubbles, through the ground in heavy strokes of bone, of skin stretched tight, through reeds and leaves and earth and water so we create, sense, become part of, are the music to which we live, breathe, move.

The Orb moves to the music it makes – trees bend, branches sway, tall grasses ripple, water stands tall, trembles splits and breaks and in the moves of the life around us we, the Body Audience, find movement to reflect. The sweeping grace of saplings and branches in the wind give us elegance as we raise our arms and bend with them. Springing from our bodies come the stories of our ancestors, our folktales, and our legends. Replications of animals on the plains, prairies, veldts, jungles, forests, seas, and sky, abstract replications of the interior churning of life as we move, as we dance, as the music dances with us and we dance with the music, with nature, with others, with ourselves.

And dance needs light. Leaping and swaying under the Sun with feet kicking dust, mud or sand; bodies twisting and baying under the

Moon with toes lifting fallen leaves or digging into the grass to find balance, light plays the Body Audience like a violin. Clichéd, yes, but aptly clichéd – as beams follow each movement, each thrust of muscle and sinew that brings forth beauty from the sweat and the agony. A gesture of sublime delicacy calls tears from the watching eyes. The World's Dance calls forth more and there in the light, the movement, the colour is a hand reaching for charcoal, burned wood, minerals - graphite, pigments - and begins to fashion Image. Holding still the kill, the life, the hunt, the birth, the celebration, the mourning, the sacred, the desecration, and the comment on such tableaux that stayed locked behind the eyes of those who saw, then drew, the minute yet monumental moments that made histories, great or small.

The dancer has been captured in picture, the actor held in the aspic of filmic time, their images given and taken in a symbiotic act and they know they have been so captured and the knowing changes the observed. Think of a woman, standing in pose to be drawn, painted, hung in her beauty in a gallery for others to see. She knows she is being gazed upon, will be gazed upon, as she looks out at us looking in at her. And, as she stands in the glow cast by the rich red curtains behind her she flushes, blushes in the opulence of colour and fabric textures, revels in knowing that there, at her back, is an intensity of hue and lushness that makes her magnificent in her knowledge of being observed.

How could she know that, so vibrant as it is, or so delicate, so bright or so pale, soothing, warning, joyous or sad in the eye of the beholder colour is but an illusion with added thoughts. Beginnings and ends. There, on that tiny, rebellious, joyous, doomed orb there is more space in the heads of man than out here

where I have never seen or sensed another being

They must exist, for do not the child-orbs live
and die out here? They cannot – do not –must
not - be alone. Surely?

Down there, on that spinning child, I was once
a creature. Well, I have been many creatures
and notice that, oddly, from one ingredient -
one ribbon of the firmament - comes rich di-
versity. The orb-child is jubilant.

I am increasingly curious.

Why?

I have tasted many lives, but those I loved
most belonged to the creature known, eventu-
ally, as Man. I was there as they became men,
and I grew to love them, envy them, be part of
them; I have been a badawī – a desert dweller
– and a television gardener. I have been a man
many times, I have been a woman many times,
I have been a eunuch many times, I have been
achingly, painfully old, and cold, frightened,

squashed and newborn. I have been a grand-mother and mother, a grandfather and father, a baby, a child, a virgin and a whore and so much more, so many times and I never tire. Yet now my wonderful, dancing, rebellious child-orb has questioned my right to live among them all…

'You have observed, joined, given them ideas. You have brought forth children from your loins, loins which are never, can never be, fully mortal.' The Orb said, 'How can I know now how they would have grown had you not joined with them? Has your view, your plea-sure, harmed them, changed them? How can I know?'

And, of course, there is no knowing. But there are things that can be known, though the knowing itself maybe too much for, or the sav-ing of, those children of the Orb, my Orb. **

There it finished, this fragment of a first chapter. The woman repacked the box, hesitated and then pulled from her bag an envelope. On it, her brother's name in her father's writing. It was sealed, once with the usual envelope gum and once with a blob of old red sealing wax. It was definitely not meant for her eyes. She ran her thumbnail around the seal, put the envelope in the box and re-tied it, looked out of the window. Then she began to gather her things; she was home. It was raining on the tail end of the afternoon, as it should be, she thought, on this day she finally bade farewell to all the physical remains of her father's life. She hoped that, all in all, he had found more joy than pain.

The following day, the woman carried a parcel from her cottage to the post office in the village high street. Such an English village is this, with thatched roofs on the cottages and the two pubs, a church and a chapel, a village store, a chemist and a doctors' surgery. There was even

a dentist. But the woman went to the post office, pausing to slip a letter into the slot in the
bright red, dome-topped pillar-box outside; her
father's lover had always had a letter from him
on her birthday, and the woman thought the
tradition should continue. A different kind of
letter, but a letter with affection and good
wishes from her would be better, she hoped,
than a gap on the doormat when the postman
called.

Inside, she posted a parcel to America. A parcel
containing the manuscript fragment, the letter
with the red sealing wax still unmarked, a letter from herself, and all of the photographs but
two: one snap of a little boy and his father on a
beach and another of a man, a celebrated author, in a silver frame. Those she saved for herself.

That done, she walked home again to await the
arrival of the desk, chair, and the boxes of
books, all to be absorbed into her own life.

As the woman walked home a young man, over three hundred miles away, was preparing lunch for his visiting family. The heat was almost liquid, as sometimes it can be down in the far west in June: a golden, mirage-infested pool of sunlight caught in the fold of cliff, house and the dip of the lower lawn and settled, like mercury. Elsewhere, on the beach below the cliff, on the upper lawn, on the banks above which the tennis courts mouldered, unused, there was a slight movement in the earthbound, heavy firmament. Not a breeze, exactly, but a sense of the sea beyond breathing; Cornwall, alive and somnolent.

Here, in the bowl of the lower lawn, ponds and swimming pool, the breath passed above heads lolling against heat-exhausted shoulders as the young man brought out the food. He and his guests – his brother, sister-in-law and small nephew - sprawled inelegantly at the garden table, growing sticky, hot, and lethargic, trying to avoid putting their elbows into any of the salads.

The small gathering was shaded by a huge, fringed canvas gazebo that covered them all easily and, with all the sides looped back, they could enjoy the views and inhale the sweet, syrupy air, though it was too thick to breathe with ease. Still, they shared a plate of spicy chicken wings, cooling each mouthful with a sip of cold beer while the child, who at three years old was just like his father had been at that age, fell asleep on a rug beside his mother's chair.

The house has not changed much since their childhood – his and his brother's – it remained a beautiful art deco Spanish villa, a hybrid creation with adaptations for coastal living. All the lawns were manicured; croquet was the outdoor summer game of choice. The pool was tiled, clean, gleaming and blue, the changing rooms in their Spanish arc around it a white, spider-free haven for towels and wet costumes, protected from the curious by oak doors.

And all this he had painted: views and seabirds, house and portraits. The young man captured them on canvas and felt himself a slave to the house, the land, his past and his memories. Yet whenever he left, he always returned, pulled by the very soil, the eyes of the house watching him wherever he roamed, never allowing him to stay away too long.

But right now, he was happy and at ease. He looked across at the mouth of the river, at the red sails of a Cornish Crabber as it slid gently up-river and thought that tomorrow he would be in his studio, his three young models and their mother posed….his phone rang and he answered lazily. No models tomorrow. The triplets had eaten too much party food, which meant he could, with a clear conscience, work on his triptych – a secular study of colour, a statement in paint – red paint - on hyponymy.

He thought with delight of sensual scarlet, of vermilion, carmine, and crimson - all hyponyms of red (their hypernym), which is, in turn, a hyponym of colour. His triptych worshipped colour, and the connections between colour…he smiled but no one saw, they were all asleep.

While the young man and his family sleep, a man in a different part of the country is busy. He is cleaning, hanging curtains, arranging flowers in vases and baking bread and cakes. His garden is pristine, his house will, he is determined, soon sparkle and by nightfall, it does. The next morning he wakes and makes himself a pot of tea and a bowl of cereal in his sunny kitchen; the news channel blurs in the background because he is not listening. He must hurry.

He is a tall, lean, neat man with a carefully trimmed mane of silver hair leaping back from his high, tanned forehead, his teeth are white and strong as he bites into his toast and his still very blue eyes scan the surfaces for his glasses – he needs them now to read and drive – and having found them he sits, enjoys his tea as he ponders the day to come. Then, with a glance at the television he checks the time against his watch, turns off the set, washes the dishes, goes upstairs to shave, shower, and dress then comes down with car keys at the ready.

He will be early, but rather that than late. He hooks his wire-framed glasses over his ears, settles them comfortably on his nose and steps from his hallway into his garage.

The car, cleaned, checked, gas tank full, runs smoothly as he backs out, idling nicely as he jumps out to close the white metal up and over door. There is a gizmo for closing it automatically but it is broken and the system is as yet unrepaired. He slides back into the driving seat and winds down his window, breathing in the mixed scents of cows and jasmine and listening to the blackbird sing in the hedgerow before he pulls carefully into the lane, and from there to the road.

He is on his way, and he is singing along to the radio, at peace with his world but still excited, happy, and hoping the day will end with him still feeling this way. He is old enough, though, to make the most of every moment of delight and right now he is delighted, so he drives extra carefully along the country roads, enjoying the early morning sunlight on the green fields, passing horses running with foals at their feet, kicking up their heels for joy in this glorious day. Joining the motorway he glories in the flowers on the embankments, swears at inept driving – not his own - and adds his baritone voice to a selection from Les Miserables as he drives.

Then, it is time to concentrate. The city, the traffic, is eating his countryside but he guides his car with precision into the maelstrom, to arrive without incident, without worry.

He found her easily; a thin, dark haired girl with a sombre cast to her face and shining dark eyes standing alone, trying to lift her bags and suitcases. Beaming he waved his a panama hat with its thin, dark red band around it and she dropped her luggage to run forward into the biggest, warmest hug of her life.

Later, after exclaiming at the beauty – at the green jewel of a meadow, at the sight of deer running across parkland, at the deep, ever changing blues of the sea as he drove along the coast road for her delight - of the countryside, he took her for lunch in an English pub. She ate a ploughman's with every sign of enjoyment, drank a half a pint of good real Ale and wandered round looking at the hunting prints, the horse brasses and the well polished oak panels.

'My granddaughter,' he said to the barman, 'From America.'

They smiled at each other, understanding the unsaid.

Finally, he brought her to his house in the village, surrounded by farmland with, if one stood on a chair at the upstairs bedroom window, a view of the sea. He showed her round, showed where things were and went to get her luggage while she, on instruction, made coffee but still managed to help him with the heaviest of the bags. They laughed a lot, then he left her unpacking in her room and she shed a tear for the old man's kindness.

He had prepared her room with care, setting up a desk and a computer, a television, a wardrobe and a dressing table as well as a chest of drawers and a bookcase. He had left her freighted boxes of well-loved books open there for her to rediscover and the entire room was painted pale blue and white with rich, dark red curtains, bedding, a well-padded easy chair and a soft rug on the dark wood floor. Now, having shared a relaxing hour with him in his garden, with their mugs of coffee, she explored the cottage while he fixed an evening meal. Coming into the dining room, where she had laid the table, he placed a bowl of fruit, a bowl of pasta salad and an assortment of dressings in glass bottles in the centre and watched as she tilted her head, looking at the painting on the wall. She liked the shades of red and pink in the sunset, the cool blues of the evening clad cliffs… she would discover, as they ate, that he had bought it in Cornwall during a holiday. Not given to mementoes, he rarely succumbed to retail impulses when he travelled but this time, drawn by the shadows, by the way the work seemed to be more an exploration of shade and tone than depiction, he had bought it, and loved it. They talked about art, then talked about her future, her new life back in the country of her birth, and decided on the adventures planned for the next few days and then, uncertain in this new place but already easing into its rhythms, she yawned her way to the luxury of a soft, static, private bed.

It was such a relief to have no-one next to her, no people around her, a bed not a tipped back seat that she was asleep within minutes and never saw him peep in, nod his satisfaction and take the hot chocolate he had made for her back to the kitchen, or knew that he sat beside his fire reading while outside the night cooled, until he heard a car. She slept through the quiet smuggling of this new arrival into the guest room, was not even awoken by the final silence of the night, owned now by owls and foxes with the inky sky domed over it all.

The woman had rearranged her study, tucking her pine computer table into a convenient corner and keeping her father's desk and chair – as he had always kept them, though never in this room – facing the door. Here she would sit when she marked papers or read. There she would sit when she wrote, or dipped into the net, researching her novels and her lecture materials. She had hung new curtains - primrose yellow to tint the light with sunshine even on a grey day - put a new yellow rug onto the old oak floor and now, clad in dusty jeans and torn red shirt she went to answer the shrill scream of the doorbell.

There stood a man with a neat mane of silver hair; he was wearing a pristine pale grey suit and his left hand rested on the shoulder of the young girl – a shy, dark haired girl – at his side. The woman noticed his carefully pared, shining nails as he explained he was her mother's father, that the girl with him was her mother's last, and again unexpected, child now orphaned and alone. She invited them inside, into the study, her face a white mask hiding her thoughts and reactions.

Uneasily, made awkward by this unreadable response, he explained that her father had left letters for them all, and he had these letters… letters they were to open together. He placed them, side by side, on her father's – on her – desk. The woman recognised the red seals, just as the girl, who had slipped silently outside, returned leading by the hand a large, dark-faced man.

Her brother. The famous author.

'Is it alright? Grandpa said I was to come.' he said and she saw inside the man a boy of twelve, gangly and full of uncertainty. Tears ran down her cheeks, her smile was a brilliant beam, the crystal beads she had caught at the curtains edging sent tiny, perfect rainbows spiralling across the walls.

'It's fine.' She said, 'It's fine.'

And she opened her arms to this sister, this brother, and this soon-to-be-beloved grandfather while her hip pressed against the edge of her father's desk.

ABOUT THE AUTHORS

Gill Kingsland

After many years as a writer of features for magazines and newspaper supplements Gill went back to University and earned an M.A in Studies in Fiction, developing an interest in history in literature, in narrative time and in reader/author interaction. She has produced a number of short stories for inclusion in ABC (the American, British and Canadian Studies academic journal, edited by the Academic Anglophone Society of Romania) and at present is working on a novel, "a spy story with more twists than Hampton Court maze."

Rhiannon Hopkins

Rhiannon has a lifelong passion for words and language. She has been published in literary magazines in England and the USA, had short stories included in anthologies by the Women's Press and poetry published in various places. She was shortlisted for the Asham Award in 2008. Rhiannon taught a creative writing class for the mental health charity Mind for three years and believes that creativity is innate, not reserved for the gifted few. She is currently working on various projects "including the novel that has haunted me for the past twenty five years."

Together Gill and Rhiannon, as Slantwise Creativity, teach creative writing workshops with a difference, seeking news ways of looking at words and language in order to deepen relationship with the creative self. You can learn more at their website www.slantwisecreativity.com

Printed in Great Britain
by Amazon